Logical Form

M000101034

Linguistic Inquiry Monographs
Samuel Jay Keyser, general editor

Logical Form   Robert May

Its Structure and
Derivation

The MIT Press
Cambridge, Massachusetts
London, England

Second printing, 1986
© 1985 by Robert May

All rights reserved. No part of this book may be reproduced in any form by any electronic or mechanical means (including photocopying, recording, or information storage and retrieval) without permission in writing from the publisher.

This book was set in Times New Roman by Asco Trade Typesetting Ltd., Hong Kong, and printed and bound by Murray Printing Co. in the United States of America.

Library of Congress Cataloging in Publication Data

May, Robert, 1951–
    Logical form.

    (Linguistic inquiry monographs; 12)
    Bibliography: p.
    Includes index.
    1. Generative grammar.   2. Language and logic.
I. Title.   II. Series.
P158.M38   1985   415   85-206
ISBN 0-262-13204-4
ISBN 0-262-63102-4 (pbk.)

Contents

Contents

Series Foreword

We are pleased to present this monograph as the twelfth in the series *Linguistic Inquiry Monographs*. These monographs will present new and original research beyond the scope of the article, and we hope they will benefit our field by bringing to it perspectives that will stimulate further research and insight.

Originally published in limited edition, the *Linguistic Inquiry Monograph* series is now available on a much wider scale. This change is due to the great interest engendered by the series and the needs of a growing readership. The editors wish to thank the readers for their support and welcome suggestions about future directions the series might take.

Samuel Jay Keyser
for the Editorial Board

Acknowledgments

It is a pleasure to thank the following friends and colleagues who have contributed in various ways and degrees (but undoubtedly more than any one of them realizes) to the development and clarification of the ideas presented here. Each made me think more deeply and carefully, and I am indebted to all of them: Noam Chomsky, Jacqueline Guéron, Jim Higginbotham, Osvaldo Jaeggli, Masaru Kajita, Hans Kamp, Ruth Kempson, Ernie Lepore, Peter Ludlow, David Pesetsky, Tanya Reinhart, Ken Safir, and Jean-Roger Vergnaud.

Special thanks are due to Professor Akira Ota for giving me the opportunity to present much of this material in lectures at the Graduate School of Languages and Linguistics of Sophia University, Tokyo. That audience, along with those at the linguistics departments of the University of Connecticut at Storrs and the University of Massachusetts at Amherst, NELS XIII at the Université du Québec à Montréal, the Levels of Grammatical Representation colloquium at the Faculté des Sciences de Luminy, the Tokyo Linguistics Seminar at the International Christian University, and the Formal Linguistics Circle of Kyoto and Nagoya, provided most receptive forums, and I have benefited greatly from the questions and criticisms they posed.

Chapter 1, "Logical Form as a Level of Linguistic Representation," is a substantially revised version of an article distributed by the Indiana University Linguistics Club.

Logical Form

Chapter 1
Logical Form as a Level of Linguistic Representation

What is the relation of a sentence's *syntactic* form to its *logical* form? This issue has been of central concern in modern inquiry into the semantic properties of natural languages at least since Frege and Russell's disagreement over definite descriptions. Frege was at pains to show how natural language deviated from the logical perfectability of his *Begriffschrift*, holding, for example, that the grammar of natural language did not properly represent the semantic structure of quantified sentences. Russell concurred with this assessment and extended the point to definite descriptions, arguing that their logical form was obfuscated by the grammar even more thoroughly, so as to require their "elimination" in logical representation. Frege, however, maintained otherwise; descriptions were akin not so much to quantifiers as to arguments, syntactically and semantically comparable, aside from their presuppositions, to proper names. Hence, in this case, the relation of form and interpretation was rather direct for Frege, in that the grammar revealed more or less transparently the logical structure of descriptions, but not so for Russell, who felt that the grammar disguised their true semantic nature.

Since that time it has become a common and traditional supposition in discussions of the relation of linguistic form to its interpretation that the grammar of a natural language, in ultimately mediating between sound and meaning, provides for a mapping from syntactic structures onto logical representations, the latter the objects of formal semantic analysis. As Donald Davidson puts it, "It would be strange if the structure essential to an account of truth were not effectively tied to the patterns of sound we use to convey truth." In this volume I will be exploring a particular approach to this view, in which the role of the grammar in characterizing semantically relevant structural properties of natural languages is explicated in terms of formal levels of grammatical representation, an approach expressed in the earliest discussions of transformational grammar, for example in Chomsky's *Syntactic Structures*:

What we are suggesting is that the notion of "understanding a sentence" will be explained in part in terms of the notion of "linguistic level." To understand a sentence, then, it is first necessary to reconstruct its analysis on each linguistic level; and we can test the adequacy of a given set of abstract linguistic levels by asking whether or not grammars formulated in terms of these levels enable us to provide a satisfactory analysis of the notion of "understanding." (p. 87)

What I will propose is that the levels of linguistic representation be articulated so as to include a level of representation, *Logical Form* (LF), related to (more precisely, derived from) other linguistic levels in specified ways. Logical Form, in the sense to be developed, will then simply be that level of representation which interfaces the theories of linguistic form and interpretation. On this view, it represents whatever properties of syntactic form are relevant to semantic interpretation—those aspects of semantic structure that are expressed syntactically. Succinctly, the contribution of grammar to meaning.

Two basic questions immediately arise. First, exactly how is this semantically relevant level of representation to be formally defined? Second, how are structures at this level assigned "meanings"; for our purposes, loosely put, under what conditions can a logical representation be said to truthfully describe, or correspond to, some appropriately individuated aspect of the world, or perhaps more accurately, of our knowledge and belief about the world? Of course, the answers to these questions are intimately intertwined, but conceptually the former, syntactic issue is prior: If there are no representations, then there is nothing to be interpreted, at least in the sense of a formal semantic interpretation. Indeed, the more highly articulated the syntactic properties of logical representations—to us, representations at LF—the more highly determined will be the interpretations such representations receive. Moreover, the more highly determined semantic structure is by syntactic structure, the more "transparent" the relation of form and interpretation will be. The question then is, just how much of the semantic structure of a natural language is manifest in its syntax? In answering this, we must consider in detail the first issue posed above.

Since the earliest work in generative grammar, an empirical goal has been to provide a class of descriptive levels for grammatical analysis, each constituted by a class of formal representations, well-formed with respect to individually necessary and collectively sufficient conditions on class membership. A *grammar* is understood as a function that specifies for each sentence of a language its formal description at each level of representation. A grammar (strongly) *generates* a class of *structural descriptions*, whose members are sets of representations $\{a_1, \ldots, a_n\}$, where each a_j $(1 \le j \le n)$ is a representation at level A_j. A "grammatical" sentence, then, is one that is assigned a structural description each of whose members are well-formed; an ungrammatical sentence is one that is assigned a structural description with at least one ill-formed member. A sentence is n-ways grammatically ambiguous if it is assigned n distinct well-formed structural descriptions.

Uncovering the properties of any hypothesized level centers around three basic concerns. One has to do with the formal nature of representations at that level, the second with how these representations are derived, and the third with constraints on their well-formedness. Though the answers to these questions will be deeply interconnected for any given level, only with respect to specified assumptions concerning rules, representations, and conditions can levels be initially individuated and their empirical content—what they represent— ultimately determined.

Let us take an example of the sort of approach I have in mind. D(eep)-Structure is the level of representation projected from lexical properties in accordance with certain conditions determining well-formedness, for example, $\overline{X}$-theory (Chomsky (1981)). S(urface)-Structure is then the level of representation derived by rules having D-Structure phrase-structure representations as their input. From a further assumption, namely that these rules effect a transformational mapping, it follows that S-Structure is a level of *phrase-structure* representation, since transformations map phrase-markers onto phrase-markers. Among the well-formedness conditions applying to S-Structure is Case-theory, in the sense of Chomsky (1980, 1981), Rouveret and Vergnaud (1980), and others, from which it follows that lexical noun phrases may occur only in positions of Case assignment. This differentiates *It is unclear what Bill is doing* from the ungrammatical **It is unclear what Bill to do*; subjects of tensed clauses are assigned nominative Case, but subjects of infinitives are usually assigned no Case at all. Thus, the grammar assigns a well-formed structural description only to the former sentence. Representations at S-Structure are, in turn, phonologically interpreted—assigned phonetic values—by rules that are, in part, sensitive to structural properties of this level. To take a well-known example, the possibility of phonologically contracting *want* and *to* to form *wanna*, as in *Who do you wanna visit*, has been argued to depend upon properties of syntactically represented empty categories, and in particular upon the Case properties assigned to these categories at S-Structure

(Jaeggli (1980b)). In this regard, S-Structure properties in part determine the sound structure assigned to a sentence, and S-Structure may be thought of as the contribution of the theory of linguistic form (that is, the syntax) to the theory of linguistic sounds.

In part, then, Universal Grammar specifies the constitution of the "core" levels of syntactic representation, now considered to include, in addition to D-Structure and S-Structure, a level of Logical Form. Extending our mode of inquiry to this latter level, we proceed as before by fixing its syntactic properties and the type of interpretations assigned to its representations. As a point of departure, then, let us suppose that representations at LF are derived by rules having S-Structure representations as their input, so that the core levels of representation are as depicted in (1), constituting the syntactic component of what has been called "sentence grammar":

(1) D-Structure—S-Structure—Logical Form

D-Structure is projected from the lexicon; it represents syntactically the basic functional and structural properties associated with lexical items. S-Structure is derived by a (possibly null) set of applications of transformational rules and in turn maps onto LF, the latter level consisting of a class of fully indexed phrase-markers. In May (1977) I proposed that the latter mapping is also transformational. From this it follows that LF is a level of phrase-structure representation as well, consisting of a class of bracketings labeled with linguistic categories, a consequence of the structure-preserving nature of transformational mappings. By hypothesis, S-Structure representations are assigned phonological interpretations, while it is to LF-representations that semantic interpretations are assigned.

To be more specific about the nature of transformational mappings, I will assume, following Chomsky (1981), that there is but one transformational rule, "Move α": Displace an arbitrary constituent to any other structural position. Among the structures that may be so derived is (2), derived by movment of the *wh*-phrase to COMP:

(2) $[_{S'} [_{COMP}$ who$_2]$ $[_S$ did John see $[_{NP}$ $e_2]]]$

The functioning of "Move α" will in all cases leave a *trace*, (designated by "e"), which is a category devoid of lexical content coindexed with, and hence bound to, the moved phrase. As for LF, "Move α" chiefly figures in its derivation in transforming the S-Structure representations of quantified sentences like *John saw everyone* into LF-representations like (3):

(3) $[_S [_{NP}$ everyone$_2]$ $[_S$ John saw $[_{NP}$ $e_2]]]$

(3) is derived by (Chomsky)-adjunction of the S-Structure object NP to the S node.[1] This central case of LF-movement, which I will refer to as QR, following the usage of May (1977), derives representations that structurally overlap in certain important ways with *wh*-constructions like (2). In particular, both contain traces coindexed with phrases displaced to positions outside the predicate's argument positions. These positions will be referred to as $\bar{A}$-*positions*, as opposed to *A-positions* (roughly, those bearing grammatical relations). Given this, we can recognize both (2) and (3) as containing (logical) variables, which, at a first approximation, are simply those traces contained within A-positions that are $\bar{A}$-bound (that is, coindexed with phrases in $\bar{A}$-positions; see Borer (1981), Chomsky (1981)). In turn, the structural properties of (2) and (3) allow us to syntactically characterize certain semantically relevant concepts. Thus, *scope* can be defined as follows:[2]

(4) The *scope* of α is the set of nodes that α c-commands at LF.

Thus, in a structure like (5a) ($= (2)$),

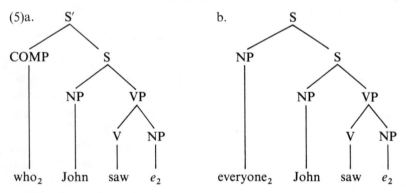

(5)a.   b.

the *wh*-phrase in COMP has scope over all the nodes it c-commands, that is, S and all the nodes S dominates. This includes the trace of *who*; hence, we may take this variable as a *bound* variable since it lies within the scope of a coindexed *wh*-phrase, interpreted here as a quasi-quantifier.[3] Parallel comments hold for representations in which the binding phrase is a true quantified phrase, as in (5b) ($= (3)$).

The grammar, then, provides for a direct representation of quantificational structure, arguing on syntactic grounds for a particular way of representing natural language quantification, although other types of representation giving rise to the same class of interpretations can be easily imagined. This is afforded to a large extent through the mediation of trace theory. As a result, it becomes possible to explain a range of phenomena by appeal to general principles of syntactic well-formedness that interact to determine the distribution and binding of lexically empty categories, where in part this generality is expressed by their holding of LF-representations. To take a simple example, it is a consequence of trace theory of movement rules that "downgrading" movements are proscribed (Fiengo (1977), May (1981)). Thus, even though relevant subcategorization restrictions are satisfied, (6) is ill-formed, since the trace is not c-commanded by the *wh*-phrase with which it is coindexed:

(6) *$[_S e_2$ wondered $[_{S'}$ who$_2$ $[_S$ Angleton suspected Philby]]]

Similarly, QR could apply so as to downgrade a phrase:

(7) *$[_S e_2$ believed $[_S$ someone$_2$ $[_S$ Angleton suspected Philby]]]

However, (7) is ill-formed for just the same reason as (6):the trace is not c-commanded by its antecedent.[4] This allows us to explain why *Someone believed Angleton suspected Philby* may only be construed with the quantifier understood as outside the scope of *believe*; it only has the well-formed LF-representation in (8):

(8) $[_S$ someone$_2$ $[_S e_2$ believed $[_S$ Angleton suspected Philby]]]

This is an indication of the initial plausibility of proposing that Universal Grammar makes available a class of conditions that determine in part not only the properties of overt movements such as *wh*-movement, but also the properties of "LF-movements" like QR that also derive structures containing traces.

The extended degree of structural articulation found at LF allows as well for the statement of generalizations not apparently manifest at other syntactic levels. One rather widely discussed case is "weak crossover" phenomena: the impossibility of construing the pronoun as anaphoric in either *Who did his mother see* or *His mother saw everyone*, although such a construal is possible with a nonquantified antecedent, as in *His mother saw John*. Given that the relevant representations are as follows,

(9)a. $[_{S'}$ who$_2$ $[_S$ did his mother see e_2]]
   b. $[_S$ everyone$_2$ $[_S$ his mother saw e_2]]
   c. $[_S$ his mother saw John]

a descriptive generalization is apparently that a trace cannot be the antecedent of a pronoun to its left; see Chomsky (1976), Higginbotham (1980), and, for somewhat different approaches, Reinhart (1983), Koopman and Sportiche (1982), and Safir (1984), as well as the discussion in chapter 5 of this volume. In (9a) the trace arises from "Move α" applying in the mapping from D-Structure to S-Structure; in (9b) it arises from "Move α" applying from S-Structure to LF. To (9c) "Move α" has not applied at all, so, in the relevant respects, its representations at D-Structure, S-Structure, and LF are nondistinct. Since the object NP is a full lexical NP, it is not proscribed from being the antecedent of the pronoun by the generalization in question. Notice that the S-Structure representations of (9a–c) would not afford the relevant generalization, since the S-Structure representation of (9b), like that of (9c), contains not a trace but a lexical object.

Having spelled out to some degree our syntactic assumptions, we now sketch the semantic assumptions underlying our primarily syntactic investigations, so as to be able to isolate the semantic properties that will intersect with the syntax of LF-representations, in particular with our notions of variable and scope. Simplifying from the approach developed in Higginbotham and May (1981a), suppose there is a (nonnull) domain D. A quantifier Q is interpreted by a *quantification* $\mathbf{Q}$ on D, a function from subsets of D onto $\{1, 0\}$ (i.e., truth and falsity).[5] *Restricted quantifications* on D, which are typically found in natural languages, differ in that they are functions from the Cartesian product of the power set of D onto $\{1, 0\}$. Restricted quantifications of the form

$$\mathbf{Q}(X, Y) = 1 \text{ iff } \psi$$
$$= 0 \text{ otherwise,}$$

where ψ is some function from X and Y onto subsets of D, interpret representations at LF of the form

$$[_\alpha Q\text{--}X_i^n [_\beta \ldots e_i \ldots]],$$

where Q ranges over quantifier elements like *every, some, few, several, so, the, a, no, two,* etc., X^n is an n-level projection of a lexical category, and β is an open sentence containing e_i free. That β is the maximal domain containing e_i free follows from assuming that a quantifier's scope coincides with its c-command domain. A quantification, then, effects a partitioning of the universe, its application to an LF-representation containing a quantifier Q being fixed by simple rule; the value of X is determined on the basis of X^n, that of Y on the basis of β. Supposing that there is an (extensional) category-type correspondence such that both X^n and β denote subsets of the domain, then $\mathbf{Q}$ establishes that relationship that must hold between X and Y, the sets so denoted, for truth to obtain. Multiple quantification sentences, whose syntax we will turn to in the next chapter, will be treated in the usual way via truth relative to an assignment of values to variables.[6]

As an example, consider the sentence *No Russian is a spy*, which has the LF-representation (10) in the relevant respects:

(10) $[_S[_{NP}$ no $[_{N'}$ Russian$]]_i$ $[_S$ e_i is a spy$]]$

This is interpreted by a quantification in which ψ is an intersective function on subsets of D:

$\textbf{No}(X, Y) = 1$ iff $X \cap Y = \emptyset$
$\qquad = 0$ otherwise.

When this quantification is applied to (10), the value of X will be fixed as

$\{x|$ Russian $(x)\}$,

while that of Y will be

$\{y|$ spy $(y)\}$.

(10) will be true, then, just in case the set of Russians and the set of spies have no members in common, and false otherwise. Similarly, the truth-conditions for other quantifiers can be specified. *Every* will be interpreted by the intersective quantification

$\textbf{Every}(X, Y) = 1$ iff $X = X \cap Y$
$\qquad = 0$ otherwise,

whereas *some* will be interpreted by

$\textbf{Some}(X, Y) = 1$ iff $X \cap Y \neq \emptyset$
$\qquad = 0$ otherwise,

which is also intersective. Numerals will be interpreted by quantifications of the form

$\textbf{n}(X, Y) = 1$ iff $|X \cap Y| = n$
$\qquad = 0$ otherwise.

This interprets the "exactly" sense of numerical quantifiers; the "at least" sense is arrived at by substituting "$\geq$," the "at most" sense by substituting "$\leq$." All three quantifications apply equally well (in the absence of any pragmatic constraint) to the LF-representation of *Three professors left*, which will then be true under three related, but distinct, interpretations pertaining to the cardinality of the intersection of the set of individuals who are professors and who left. *The* will be interpreted by

$\textbf{The}(X, Y) = 1$ iff $X = X \cap Y = \{a\}$, for $a \in D$
$\qquad = 0$ otherwise,

which embeds the existence and uniqueness properties of definite descriptions, found invariantly under alternative scopes:

(11) The president of every public authority in New York is a crook.

Although on the preferred construal of (11) *the* has narrower scope, it can also have broader scope, a construal facilitated by substituting *Robert Moses* for *a crook*. On the former interpretation (11) entails that each authority has one, and only one, president; on the latter it entails that there is exactly one person who is president of all the public authorities. This is as expected, since these properties of interpretation do not accrue to *the* in virtue of its scope. We are thus distinguishing properties of quantifiers traceable to structural sources from those that are lexically inherent, expressed as aspects of quantifications. Indeed, this can be the only source of inherent properties of quantifiers, since syntactic rules—and in particular transformational mappings, including those onto LF—are context-free and hence blind to lexical governance. This precludes the possibility of marking quantifiers for specified scopes, although inherent properties may be more consonant with certain scopes. For example, *each* often preferentially takes broad scope. But whatever the source of this preference, we would not want to maintain that it is an obligatorily broad scope quantifier, for it can have narrow scope as well, as in (12), in which it stands inside the embedded quantifier in LF:

(12) Each person in some midwestern city voted for Debs in the '08 election.

Thus, the theory sharply distinguishes the general grammatical properties of quantifiers—their scope—from their lexical properties, expressed semantically by quantifications.

The set-theoretic interpretation of quantifiers just sketched constitutes an hypothesis regarding the semantic component of our linguistic knowledge of quantification. Now, of course, our syntactic assumptions do not uniquely determine the sort of semantics just outlined; one could imagine other interpretive systems wedded to the structural aspects of LF. But whatever the exact system of semantic interpretation assumed, insofar as it characterizes notions that interact with grammatically determined semantic structure, we will have an argument that linguistic theory should countenance a formal semantic component with those properties. To take an example, the notion of quantification adumbrated above allows us to classify quantifiers as either monotone increasing or monotone decreasing, depending upon whether they warrant upward or downward entailments between pairs like (13a)/(13b) and (13a)/(13c) (Barwise and Cooper (1981)):

(13)a. Every man left.
  b. Every father left.
  c. Every man left early.

(13a) entails (13b); this is a downward entailment, since it runs from a superset, the set of men, to a subset, the set of fathers. On the other hand, the entailment relation between (13a) and (13c) is upward entailing, since it runs from a subset, the set of individuals who left early, to a superset, the set of individuals who left. Thus, we will say that the quantifier *every*, interpreted by the quantification given above, is monotone decreasing for argument X and monotone increasing for Y. (What I am calling "monotone increasing/decreasing for X," Barwise and Cooper (1981) call persistent/ antipersistent, reserving the term monotone for what I have referred to as monotonicity for Y.) All other quantifiers can be classified by their monotone properties; for example, *no* is monotone decreasing for both X and Y, and *some* is monotone increasing for both.

Monotone properties of quantifiers afford a number of interesting generalizations with syntactic consequences. To mention one, apparently only quantifiers that are monotone decreasing for Y can be moved to COMP in S-Structure:[7]

(14) Only/no/few spies that he trusts would Dulles send inside Russia.

This contrasts with quantifiers that minimally differ from those in (14) in being monotone increasing for this argument:

(15) *Every/all/many spies that he trusts would Dulles send inside
      Russia.

Another very interesting case is discussed by Ladusaw (1981). He argues that a necessary condition on the occurrence of polarity *any* is that it occur within the scope of a monotone decreasing operator. He points to examples like (16), which under the assumptions made here have the LF-representations in (17):

(16)a. No student who ever read anything about phrenology attended
       Gall's lecture.
   b. No student who attended Gall's lecture had ever read anything
      about phrenology.

(17)a. no student who ever read anything about phrenology$_2$ [e_2 attended Gall's lecture]

   b. no student who attended Gall's lecture$_2$ [e_2 had ever read anything about phrenology]

In deriving (17) it has been assumed that QR applies to the entire restrictive relative clause, not just to its head. This is just as with *wh*-movement; thus, *Which book that John likes did he give to Mary to read* contrasts with **Which book did he give that John likes to Mary to read*. Thus, in (17a) the polarity item *anything* is included in the part of the logical form that fixes the value of *X* in the quantification interpreting *no*; in (17b) it is included in the part that fixes the value of *Y*. Since *no* is monotone decreasing for both arguments, occurrence of polarity items is warranted in either consitituent in the LF-representation. On the other hand, both (18a) and (18b) are ungrammatical, since *some* is fully monotone increasing:

(18)a. *Some student who ever read anything about phrenology attended Gall's lecture.

   b. *Some student who attended Gall's lecture had ever read anything about phrenology.

In contrast to (16) and (18), Ladusaw points to examples like (19):

(19)a. Every student who ever read anything about phrenology attended Gall's lecture.

   b. *Every student who attended Gall's lecture had ever read anything about phrenology.

Since *every* is monotone decreasing for *X*, and monotone increasing for *Y*, the polarity item can only occur in the part of the LF-representation corresponding to the former argument; thus, (19a) is well-formed, but not (19b).

The "pied-piping" property of QR, whose importance we have just observed in describing the properties of polarity items, has a number of other consequences. For example, VP-deletion is possible, in general, if neither the missing verb nor its antecedent c-commands the other. This will clearly always hold when VP-deletion applies across sentential conjuncts or members of a discourse. But consider (20), the case of antecedent contained deletion discussed in Sag (1976) and elsewhere:

(20) Dulles suspected everyone who Angleton did

This seems to violate the condition, since *suspected* c-commands *did*. But as

Sag and Williams (1977) have argued, the constraints on VP-deletion are properly stated over logical representations, and indeed the LF-representation of (20) will be consistent with the c-command constraint, for now there is no c-command relation. between the verb phrase headed by *suspected* and the missing VP marked by *did*:

(21) [everyone who Angleton did$_2$ [Dulles suspected e_2]]

I will suppose, along with Williams, that VP-deletion involves a reconstruction of the missing VP in the place of the pro-form, respecting certain identity conditions. Though matters are in fact somewhat more complex, it will suffice for our purposes to simply assume that it is the syntactic VP which is copied; the resulting structure will be as in (22):

(22) [[everyone who Angleton suspected e_2]$_2$ [Dulles suspected e_2]]

This represents just the desired interpretation, namely that Angleton and Dulles suspected all the same people. Note that in (22) *who* now properly binds an empty category, presuming that it is normally coindexed with the head of the relative. A comparable substitution of VP in the S-Structure of (20), however, would lead to a reconstructive regress, for substitution of the VP *everyone who Angleton did* would lead to a structure still containing a deleted VP, which itself would have to be reconstructed, and so on. That such a regress is a cause of ungrammaticality can be surmised from the deviance of (23), with a nonrestrictive relative (compare *Dulles suspected Philby, and Angleton did too*).

(23) *Dulles suspected Philby, who Angleton did

Here, since LF-movement affects only quantified phrases, there is no possibility of deriving the structure that properly permits reconstruction. Needless to say, the contrast between (20) and (23) provides strong evidence for a level of Logical Form, and for movement operations onto that level that single out quantified phrases. This is reinforced by the account of examples like (24), understood with *suspected* as the head of the deleted VP; its ungrammaticality contrasts with the well-formedness of *Dulles suspected everyone who knew Philby, and Angleton did too*, on the intended interpretation:[8]

(24) *Dulles suspected everyone who knew Philby, who Angleton did.

It might be thought that substitution of an antecedent VP in a nonrestrictive relative would be possible if it were moved as part of another phrase, so as to avoid the regress just described for (23). This is so, but, it turns out, a well-formed LF-representation still cannot be derived. Application of QR gives (25a); subsequent substitution of the VP, (25b):

(25)a. [[everyone who$_2$ knew Philby, who$_3$ Angleton did]$_2$ [Dulles suspected e_2]]

    b. [[everyone who$_2$ knew Philby, who$_3$ Angleton suspected e_2]$_2$ [Dulles suspected e_2]]

The problem with (25b) is that the embedded *wh*-phrase binds no empty category. That is, the two *wh*-phrases will bear distinct indices, but the index of the empty category contained in the reconstructed VP must be that of the higher occurrence of *who*, since only this occurrence is coindexed with the phrase that undergoes LF-movement. Thus, the ungrammaticality of (24) can be attributed to its LF-representation (25b) containing an operator that binds no variable. Note that the analysis further predicts that *Dulles suspected everyone who knew some agent who Angleton did* is grammatical, but only with an interpretation under which the deleted phrase is understood as the embedded VP, that headed by *knew*.

    The grammar thus provides sufficient structure so that at LF the application of quantifications can be transparently determined. This structure arises from assuming that LF-representations of quantified sentences are derived by transformational mappings, exploiting a notion of logically bound variable that receives grammatical foundation through trace theory. Note that such mappings do not "translate" between the *sentences* of some language and those of some other formal representational system; rather, they are mappings wholly within the formal representational system for natural language. Indeed, the assumption that LF is derived in this way adds nothing to linguistic theory that need not otherwise be assumed to be provided by UG. Thus, I am arguing that whatever theoretical apparatus is needed to properly characterize the syntactic properties of *wh*-constructions like *Who does Angleton suspect* will be sufficient to properly characterize the syntactic properties of the LF-representation of *Angleton suspected everyone*, giving a general theory of the representation of quantificational binding without introducing any special types of rules or principles. This is an important point, and it should be emphasized. Assuming that there is a level of Logical Form derived by "More α" does not entail any extension of the formal nomenclature of linguistic theory—that is, there is no extension of the types of grammatical rules or representations that it countenances—although it does extend the range of phenomena that prima facie, fall under its descriptive and explanatory purview. Insofar as this approach can be seen to be empirically motivated, then, it will

represent the best possible circumstance for incorporating a theory of
logical representation within the grammar.

We now turn to the logical syntax of multiple quantification. Although I
will come to modify this approach in chapter 2, consider as a point of
departure the following analysis, that of May (1977), of the class of
structures derived by application of QR to (26), an S-Structure representation containing two quantified phrases:

(26) $[_S[_{NP}$ every spy] $[_{VP}$ suspects $[_{NP}$ some Russian]]]

A single application of QR to either NP in (26) yields the structures in (27):

(27)a. $[_S[_{NP}$ every spy]$_2$ $[_S$ e_2 suspects $[_{NP}$ some Russian]]]
    b. $[_S[_{NP}$ some Russian]$_3$ $[_S[_{NP}$ every spy] suspects e_3]]

Since QR is a (Chomsky)-adjunction, each of these structures now contains
two S nodes to which further application of QR can attach phrases,
allowing for the derivation of the distinct structures in (28):[9]

(28)a. $[_S[_{NP}$ every spy]$_2$ $[_S[_{NP}$ some Russian]$_3$ $[_S$ e_2 suspects e_3]]]
    b. $[_S[_{NP}$ some Russian]$_3$ $[_S[_{NP}$ every spy]$_2$ $[_S$ e_2 suspects e_3]]]

(28a) and (28b) represent the ambiguity of *Every spy suspects some Russian*
as a matter of quantifier scope. Since in (28a) *every spy* c-commands *some
Russian*, but not vice versa, the former has broader scope. The opposite
holds in (28b), in which *some Russian* has been adjoined at a higher position
from which it has broader scope over *every spy*. Thus, simply given the free
application of QR (and the usual sort of assumptions about the recursive
assignment of truth-conditions), it is possible to represent certain ambiguities of multiple quantification, so that an S-Structure representation such
as (26) will count as grammatically disambiguated with respect to its logical
form.

Bear in mind that the issue of concern here is to what degree the class of
possible interpretations that can be assigned to a given syntactic structure is
a function of its grammatical properties. This is not to say, however, that
every *sentence* of a given form will exhibit every possible interpretation;
even less to say a sentence will exhibit every possible interpretation on every
use. Which construal or construals will be preferred on a given occasion of
use is a matter that goes beyond grammar per se, taking into account
various properties of discourse, shared knowledge of the interlocutors,
plausibility of description, etc.[10] To conflate these matters would be to
confuse the grammatical issue—to what degree a sentence's structure fixes

its meaning—with an issue ultimately of use. And to do so would undoubtedly not lead to a clear understanding of the content of either topic.

Sentences of mixed universal and existential quantification, such as *Everybody loves somebody*, have the property that one of the interpretations represented by their logical forms entails the other, a matter of logic, just as it is a matter of logic that the interpretations represented by the logical forms of *Everyone loves everyone* are equivalent. Regardless of these logical relations, however, both sentences are assigned two structurally distinct representations at LF; their equivalence or nonequivalence simply amounts to the claim that distinct modes of composition either do or do not lead to identical interpretations. From the logical relations of such sentences, however, another moral can be drawn, namely that there is no need to represent both scope orders; instead, only one need be represented, the other to be seen as following in virtue of some logical (or perhaps pragmatic) relation. For instance, with sentences of mixed universal and existential quantifiers, there would be only a representation of the interpretation in which the existential has broader scope, for this entails the other interpretation, in which the universal has broader scope. In a sense, this is to take the logical laws of quantification theory as generative, rather than interpretive, since they derive the interpretations not given by the grammar. On this view, however, it would seem that it remains necessary to reserve multiplicity of representation for any sentence whose interpretations are logically independent, since otherwise there would be no way to derive all its interpretations. Just this is found in sentences such as (29), which on one construal is true just in case everyone is a lover, on the other just in case everyone is loved:[11]

(29) Nobody loves nobody.

Assuming that *no* is logically glossed as the negation of the existential quantifier, the interpretations of this sentence can be schematically represented as follows:

(30)a. $- \exists x - \exists y \, P(x, y) \leftrightarrow \forall x \, \exists y \, P(x, y)$ (Everyone is a lover)
  b. $- \exists y - \exists x \, P(x, y) \leftrightarrow \forall y \, \exists x \, P(x, y)$ (Everyone is loved)

But if it is necessary to countenance an ambiguity of representation for *Nobody loves nobody*, as a matter of grammar, it is hard to see how a parallel ambiguity can be disallowed for *Everybody loves somebody*, given that they have identical S-Structure constituencies. One could invoke some sort of semantic or syntactic constraint to obtain this result, but it is unclear how the former would avoid the ill effect of constraining the functioning of grammatical rules not formally but on the basis of a sentence's meaning, [12] while the latter would have to be quite complicated in order to pick out a constant representation under varying surface positions of the particular lexical quantifiers, to which the condition would have to overtly refer. Even if some such approach were feasible, however, it would obscure the fact that there may be ambiguities of composition accruing to sentences in virtue of their syntactic construction, and it would fail to recognize the role of general syntactic rules and principles in grammatically expressing such ambiguities. But surely this is a proposition we wish to entertain, within the context of particular grammatical theories.

For multiple quantification sentences, then, representation at LF disambiguates their interpretations. Ambiguities of multiple quantification are therefore syntactic ambiguities, grammatically disambiguated, a "constructional homonymity." Such disambiguation as we find at LF, under our syntactic characterization of this level, will clearly be relevant in determining logical consequence in natural language (with respect to a specified semantic interpretation), although since LF does not represent contextually assigned values of indexical elements, for instance, or the knowledge, beliefs, and intentions of the interlocutors, matters that transcend the grammatical, it will only contribute part of the overall characterization of the structure of inference in natural language. (This is not to say that inferences involving nongrammatical factors will not make reference to LF, only to say that they will not be *represented* at this level.) LF will constitute just the grammatical component of this overall system, contributing a notion of consequence following in virtue of syntactic constituency and grammatical form. Note that there can be no a priori judgment with respect to just which inferences fall in the latter class; this is an empirical matter that can be adjudged only with respect to a fixed nexus of assumptions about the nature of syntax and its relation to semantic interpretation. For instance, it is by no means necessary to hold that ambiguities of multiple quantification are represented at any syntactic level, eschewing the assumption that the representation of quantifier scope involves movement and maintaining instead that insofar as this is represented, it is within the semantic, not syntactic, component. Part of the appeal of such a view is that it might allow for a seemingly simpler "surface" syntax; see Cooper (1983) for an account along these lines. [13] But as pointed out above, this is illusory, because assuming movement onto a syntactic level of LF does not extend the formal structure of the theory. Moreover, the motivation for LF does not arise solely from its being disambiguated, to whatever degree, but to a large extent because it extends the empirical domain of syntax so as to afford uniform accounts of a number of generalizations that might otherwise only be describable, in a theory that eschews this assumption, via a disjunction of heterogeneous properties. To take an example, consider certain basic properties of *wh*-questions. As is well known, the verbs *believe, wonder,* and *know* form a paradigm when taking finite complement clauses; *believe* takes only declarative complements, *wonder* interrogative, and *know* either. Since *believe* takes only declaratives, **Philby believed who Angleton suspected,* containing an indirect question, is ungrammatical, although direct questions with *believe* are possible: *Who did Philby believe that Angleton suspected. Wonder,* on the other hand, requires an interrogative complement: *Philby wondered who Angleton suspected,* but **Who did Philby wonder (that) Angleton suspected.* By contrast, *know* takes both types of complements, as witnessed by the grammaticality of both the direct question *Who did Philby know that Angleton suspected* and the indirect question *Philby knows who Angleton suspected.* Now suppose, as is usual, that predicates subcategorize for declarative or interrogative clauses inclusively. Marking COMP with the feature [±WH] as a convenient method for registering this, the well-formed cases just noted will have the representations in (32) through (34):[14]

(32)   who did Philby believe [$_{S'}$[$_{COMP}$ −WH that] [$_S$ Angleton suspected *e*]]

(33)   Philby wondered [$_{S'}$[$_{COMP}$ +WH who] [$_S$ Angleton suspected *e*]]

(34)a. who did Philby know [$_{S'}$[$_{COMP}$ −WH that] [$_S$ Angleton suspected *e*]]

   b. Philby knows [$_{S'}$[$_{COMP}$ +WH who] [$_S$ Angleton suspected *e*]]

As a first approximation, we can account for these observations on the basis of the following principle:

(35) *Wh*-Criterion
     a. Every [+WH] COMP must dominate a *wh*-phrase.
     b. Every *wh*-phrase must be dominated by a [+WH] COMP.

(33) and (34b) are consistent with the *Wh*-Criterion, since they contain [+WH] COMPs filled by *wh*-phrases. (32) and (34a) also satisfy this condition, since they contain [−Wh] COMPs. If a *wh*-phrase were to move into the complement COMP in either case, the resulting structures would be ruled out, since they would contain *wh*-phrases not governed by [+WH]. The effect of the *Wh*-Criterion, then, is to require *wh*-movement whenever

there is a $[+\text{WH}]$ COMP, since only then can there be the requisite containment in COMP.[15]

The examples discussed so far are neutral with respect to whether the *Wh*-Criterion holds of S-Structure or LF. If it holds of the latter, then movement of the *wh*-phrase is obligatory not only in (33) and (34b), but also in multiple questions like (36):

(36) $[_{S'}$ which spy $_2$ $[_S$ e_2 suspects $[_{NP}$ which Russian]]]

Only if the *wh*-phrase not in COMP in S-Structure is moved there in LF will the *Wh*-Criterion be satisfied. This can be accomplished by assuming that LF-movement applies to quantified expressions in general, including the quasi-quantificational *wh*-phrases found in direct and indirect questions, moving them when unmoved at S-Structure into COMP at LF. Then at LF (37) can be derived from (36) (the structure of COMP in such examples will be more exactly specified in chapters 3 and 5):

(37) $[_{S'}$ which Russian$_3$ which spy$_2$ $[_S$ e_2 suspects e_3]]

As both *wh*-phrases now occur in COMP, the *Wh*-Criterion (now taken as a condition on LF is satisfied), and (37) can be properly interpreted as a multiple question. If movement is into a COMP to which an interrogative interpretation is not assigned, the result is deviant; thus, (38) violates the *Wh*-Criterion, since there is no $[+\text{WH}]$ COMP into which the *wh*-phrase can move at LF:

(38) *The spy who suspects which Russian is Angleton.

The analysis of (37) and (38) assumes that LF-movement of a *wh*-phrase is to COMP, as in S-Structure, and as opposed to movement of other (non-*wh*) quantified phrases, which adjoin to S. This may simply reflect the more general fact, in part formally expressed by the *Wh*-Criterion, that COMP is a selected position, which can be occupied only by phrases satisfying its selectional restrictions, others being excluded.

The role of LF-movements in accounting for properties of *wh*-constructions gains further support from observations of Huang (1982a). He notes that in Chinese interrogatives, there is no overt *wh*-movement at S-Structure.[16] Thus, (39) through (41) are syntactically identical, aside from choice of matrix verb:

(39) Zhangsan xiang-zhidao [ta muqin kanjian shei].
     Zhangsan wonder   his mother see   who
     'Zhangsan wondered who his mother saw.'

(40) Zhangsan xiangxin [ta muqin kanjian shei].
     Zhangsan believe   his mother see   who
     'Who does Zhangsan believe his mother saw?'

(41) Zhangsan zhidao [ta muqin kanjian shei].
     Zhangsan know   his mother see   who
     a. 'Who does Zhangsan know his mother saw?'
     b. 'Zhangsan knows who his mother saw.'

Huang points out that the interpretations of these examples are identical to those of their English counterparts. Thus, (39) can only be understood as a direct question and (40) as an indirect question, whereas (41) is ambiguous between these construals, as indicated by the glosses.

The explanation for this, Huang argues, follows from holding that Chinese differs minimally from English in that unary questions are derived by wh-movements confined to the mapping from S-Structure onto LF. What is apparently constant in Chinese and English are the subcategorization properties of the relevant predicates. Thus, "believe" takes only [−WH] complements, "wonder" only [+WH], and "know" either. Given that the Wh-Criterion applies at LF, it now follows that the LF-representations of the Chinese examples (39) through (41) will be structurally nondistinct from those of their English counterparts in the glosses. That movement is in fact involved here is further evidenced by the fact, observed in Higginbotham (1980), that the pronouns in (39) through (41) cannot be construed as variables bound by shei; that is, they display weak crossover effects. As noted earlier, as a generalization, a variable cannot serve as antecedent of a pronoun to its left. If the derivation of the LF-representations in (39) through (41) involves movement, then the Chinese weak crossover effects can be accounted for on exactly the same grounds as their English counterparts. By assuming, then, that wh-phrases can—and in fact, given the Wh-Criterion, must—be moved to COMP in LF, the properties of LF afford a general explanation of the apparent universality of wh-complementation. Thus, we find identity of interpretation, even though only in English are direct and indirect questions structurally distinguished at S-Structure.

Huang's observations provide, I believe, a very strong prima facie case for the existence of LF-movements and hence for the level of LF itself. Another example to the same point can be made on the basis of properties of crossing coreference:

(42) Every pilot who shot at it hit some MIG that chased him.

As is well known, sentences like (42) allow for a construal in which the antecedent of *it* is taken as *some MIG that chased him* and *him* is simultaneously understood as having *every pilot who shot at it* as antecedent. The property of these sentences that is interesting here is how this pattern of crossed binding of the pronouns is to be represented at LF. First, however, it is important to consider some special properties of the anaphoric relation illustrated in (43):

(43) Every MIG destroyed its target.

As many authors have noted,[17] the pronoun in (43) is most properly construed as a bound variable; since its antecedent is not referential, anaphora here clearly cannot be explicated through co- or overlapping reference. In our terms, we may represent this construal by (44):

(44) [$_S$ every MIG$_2$ [$_S$ e_2 destroyed its$_2$ target]]

The pronoun is (properly) bound by the trace arising from movement of the quantifier phrase. There is no particular reason to suppose that the pronoun is replaced by a variable at LF, since semantically its interpretation will be wholly determined by the nature of the interpretation of the element that ultimately binds it, here a quantifier.

Now consider a somewhat more complicated example:

(45) Every pilot hit some MIG that chased him.

Like other simple transitive clauses discussed above, (45) exhibits a scope ambiguity; either quantifier may be understood as having broader scope over the other. Interestingly, the construal of the pronoun *him* varies according to the scope relations: *him* can be bound by *every pilot* only if *every pilot* is understood as having broader scope than *some MIG that chased him*. The LF-representations derivable from the S-Structure representation of (45) are those in (46):

(46)a. [every pilot$_2$ [[some MIG that chased him]$_3$ [e_2 hit e_3]]]
   b. [[some MIG that chased him]$_3$ [every pilot$_2$ [e_2 hit e_3]]]

Consider (46a). Here the pronoun resides within the scope of the c-commanding quantifier phrase *every pilot* and hence can be construed as a bound variable. In (46b), on the other hand, *him* is not within the scope of *every pilot*; the c-command domain of the latter phrase is solely the most deeply embedded S. When *some* is assigned broader scope, the pronoun is carried along to a position outside the scope of *every*. Hence, in this structure no bound variable construal of the pronoun is possible.

The relevant property of LF-representations that accounts for the range of interpretations available to (45) can be stated as follows:

(47) A pronoun is a bound variable only if it is within the scope of a coindexed quantifier phrase.

This properly accounts for the availability of a bound construal in (46a) and for its absence in (46b). That this principle holds of LF is demonstrated by the availability of a bound variable construal of the pronoun in *Somebody in every city despises it*. If the principle on bound variable anaphora held at S-Structure, we would not expect this to be possible, but, as we shall see in chapter 3, at LF the embedded quantified phrase is extracted to a position in which it c-commands the object pronoun.

Now reconsider the case of crossed binding, the "Bach-Peters" example in (42), *Every pilot who shot at it hit some MIG that chased him*. Given our assumptions so far, QR can derive two structures from the S-Structure representation of this sentence:

(48)a. [[every pilot who shot at it]$_2$ [[some MIG that chased him]$_3$
      [e_2 hit e_3]]]

   b. [[some MIG that chased him]$_3$ [[every pilot who shot at it]$_2$
      [e_2 hit e_3]]]

We are now faced with a problem. In (48a), although *him* can be construed as a bound variable, since it is c-commanded by the *every*-phrase, *it* cannot be construed in this way, since it is not c-commanded by the *some*-phrase. Just the inverse circumstance obtains in (48b); here only *it* can be a bound variable. It would seem, then, that it is not possible to represent the simultaneous binding of the two pronouns.

In Higginbotham and May (1981a, 1981b) it is argued that crossed binding sentences are to be properly analyzed as containing "binary quantifiers." The idea developed there is that among the rules applying to LF is *Absorption*, whose effect can be characterized as follows:

(49) ... [NP$_i$ [NP$_j$ ... → ... [NP$_i$ NP$_j$]$_{i,j}$ ...

Structurally, Absorption takes structures in which one NP immediately c-commands another NP and derives structures in which they form something like a conjoined constituent:

(50)

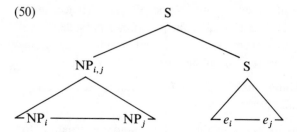

In the absorbed structure (50), NP_i c-commands NP_j and vice versa. Semantically, such structures are interpreted by binary (actually n-ary) quantifications, derived from pairs (n-tuples) of unary quantifications, defined as functions from the power set of the Cartesian product of D onto $\{0, 1\}$. This is for unrestricted binary quantifiers. Restricted binary quantifiers are functions from $P(D \times D) \times P(D \times D)$. If the binary quantification is made up of "intersective" quantifiers, that is, those that are defined in terms of intersections of subsets of D, then it can be proven that the absorbed and nonabsorbed LF-representations lead to equivalent interpretations, with the further proviso that the narrower scope quantifier contain no occurrence of x free. Thus, just the same truth-conditions will be ascribed to *Everybody loves someone*, regardless of whether it is represented at LF with absorbed quantifiers or not. Where binary quantifiers differ is that they apply to all variable positions simultaneously. Thus, they are particularly suited for the treatment of crossed binding (Bach-Peters) sentences. Both of the representations (48a) and (48b) satisfy the structural description of Absorption, deriving (51):

(51)a. [[every pilot who shot at it]$_2$ [some MIG that chased him]$_3$]$_{2,3}$
      [e_2 hit e_3]

   b. [[some MIG that chased him]$_3$ [every pilot who shot at it]$_2$]$_{2,3}$
      [e_2 hit e_3]

In both of these structures, the syntactic condition on bound variable anaphora is satisfied, because the *every*-phrase c-commands *him* and the *some*-phrase c-commands *it*. Focusing on (51a), we see that it is interpreted by the binary quantification

Every, Some$(R, S) = 1$ iff $x \in dom\ R \to (R \cap S)'\ x \neq \emptyset$
                    $= 0$ otherwise.

In the notation of Higginbotham and May (1981a), *dom R* denotes the domain of a relation R on D, and $R'\ x$ stands for

$\{y \in D | \langle x, y \rangle \in R\}.$

Applying this quantification to (51a), we set R equal to

$\{\langle x, y \rangle | x$ is a pilot who shot at y and y is a MIG that chased $x\}$

and S equal to

$\{\langle x, y \rangle | x$ hit $y\}.$

(51a) is then true iff for any pilot who shot at a MIG that chased him, there is at least one such MIG that he hit, and these truth-conditions accord with our intuitive judgment about such sentences. See Higginbotham and May (1981a) for a detailed formal development of the semantics of binary quantifiers.

From the syntactic side, an important property of this analysis of crossed binding is that it assumes that Absorption can apply only to local pairs of quantifiers. Absorption, so to speak, takes two quantifier phrases A and B such that A immediately c-commands B, but not vice versa, into a structure in which A and B c-command each other. As with wh-complementation, the approach assumes that there is LF-movement and, moreover, that the relevant properties will also be found where there is overt S-Structure movement. That is, it assumes that the application of Absorption is blind to whether quantifier A came to c-command quantifier B via application of overt movements (i.e., those onto S-Structure), covert movements (i.e., those onto LF), or some combination thereof. That this is in fact the case is borne out by following examples, all of which exhibit crossed binding:

(52)a. Which pilot who shot at it hit which MIG that chased him?
   b. Which pilot who shot at it hit some MIG that chased him?
   c. Which MIG that chased him did every pilot who shot at it hit?

Wh-movement has applied in each of these cases, so the initial wh-phrase occurs in COMP. In each case further application of QR gives a representation to which Absorption applies; in (52a) this movement is of another wh-phrase, in (52b) and (52c) a quantifier phrase. The contrast between (52b) and (52c) shows that crossed binding is possible regardless of whether the wh-phrase in COMP has been moved from subject or from object. This is just as we would expect, given the proposed analysis.

The possibility of crossed binding in these examples contrasts with a similar class of cases, brought out by Jacobson (1977), which differ in that they do not contain quantified phrases. (53) is an example:

(53) His wife saw her husband.

Unlike the previous cases, this sentence cannot receive a crossed interpretation: *his* cannot be taken as dependent upon *her husband* simultaneously with *her* being dependent on *his wife*. This is all the more odd, given the possibility of coreference in both *His wife saw John* and *Mary saw her husband*. Higginbotham and May (1981b) argue that the reason for this is that fixing the values of the pronouns in (53) turns on a particular property of reference, namely that it must be fixed in a definite, noncircular fashion. This is not possible for (53); the reference of *his* is given by *her husband*, which in turn contains a pronoun *her*, whose reference is given by *his wife*, which contains *his*, whose reference is given by *her husband*, etc. Thus, the "chain of reference" associated with this sentence is circular and unending, leading to no definite determination of reference at all. If some other phrase is available to which the referential chain can lead that does not contain a pronoun, this sort of vicious circularity is avoided; thus, there is no problem in interpreting either *His wife, Mary, saw her husband* or *His wife saw Jack, her husband*.

Assuming that there are distinct devices for the establishment of referential, as opposed to bound variable, anaphora, it is possible to account for certain cases that appear to be crossover environments, but in which an anaphoric interpretation can be easily obtained. Thus, consider the difference between the nonrestrictive relatives in the following (a) examples and the free relatives in the (b) examples:

(54)a. John, who his mother admires, ...
    b. Whoever his mother admires ...

(55)a. Stieglitz, whose picture of O'Keefe he took while she was lying supine, ...
    b. Whoever's picture of O'Keefe he took while she was lying supine, ...

That an anaphoric interpretation cannot be obtained for the pronouns in the free relatives is not surprising; these are simply cases of crossover. What is surprising is that an anaphoric interpretation *is* possible in the nonrestrictive relatives, since the *wh*-phrase, its trace, and the pronoun all stand in the same structural relation as in the free relative. An account is forthcoming, however, once it is recognized that there is an alternative route to anaphora available for the nonrestrictives not found with the free relatives. Let us suppose that the *wh*-phrase in nonrestrictives is an operator whose value is specified by the reference of the head. This much would seem to need to be incorporated in any semantic treatment of this construction. Now strictly speaking the pronoun in (54a), for instance, cannot be a bound variable, because this would violate the crossover constraint. This constraint, however, does not bar the pronoun from being referential and from picking up its reference in the manner described above for such pronouns. In particular, there is nothing to stop its picking up the reference of the head of the relative, *John*, which after all is an independent referring expression. But then the mechanisms of reference will specify the same value for the pronoun that the *wh*-phrase specifies for the variable it binds. An anaphoric interpretation therefore arises for the nonrestrictives through the mediation of mechanisms for the specification of referential values. However, these are not available for free relatives, which are headless. Rather, they may avail themselves solely of the mechanisms of quantification and bound variables, which preclude anaphora in the configuration under consideration.

Thus, we see from these latter cases, as well as from the distinction in crossed binding sentences between the sensible *Every pilot who shot at it hit some MIG that chased him* and the nonsensical *His wife saw her husband*, that there is a fundamental distinction between those pronouns that receive their values via mechanisms of quantification and those that receive them via mechanisms of assignment of reference. Thus, like all the discussion to this point, the analysis of these cases rests on the assumption that at LF quantified and nonquantified phrases are distinguished, not only in their interpretation, but also in those aspects of their syntax to which the rules of interpretation are sensitive. In this regard the position differs from that found in Montague (1974), for instance, in which quantified and nonquantified phrases are assimilated under a uniform syntactic and semantic treatment. Now insofar as the phenomena we have been discussing turn on distinguishing these types of expressions, it argues against such a conflation of categories, at least from the syntactic perspective. Indeed, given the validity of the analyses, the phenomena we have considered can be employed as a diagnostic of quantificational status. For instance, consider definite phrases, those containing *the*. Are they quantified phrases? We have assumed that they are; recall the semantic treatment of definite descriptions above. This is corroborated by their having interacting scope relations, seen in sentences such as *Every man admires the woman he loves*[18] and *The president of every public authority is a crook*; by their allowing VP-deletion in relatives, as seen in *Dulles suspected the agents who Philby did*; by their occurrence in crossed binding sentences such as *The pilot who shot at it hit the MIG that chased him*; and by the differential distribution of *any*, seen in the contrast between *The students who had ever read anything about phrenology attended Gall's lecture* and **The students who attended Gall's* *lecture had ever read anything about phrenology*. Thus, insofar as the explanation of these phenomena turns on the assumption that there is LF-movement, and insofar as LF-movement is sensitive to whether phrases are quantificational, then it follows that *the*, at least on the uses exemplified above, is a quantifier, since otherwise we would expect to find quite a different complex of properties. And it is the fact that we do find these contrasting complexes of properties that argues for the fundamental distinction of logical syntax that forms a basic presupposition of our inquiries. In this regard our position agrees with the line of thinking from Frege to Tarski, in which quantified phrases were taken to require treatment quite distinct from that of proper names.

Once we take the distinction in semantic type between quantificational and referential expressions as basic, then the syntactic paradigms found at LF can be seen as consequences of requirements on the mapping of argument structure onto logical form. Following Chomsky (1981), we will suppose that the relation of arguments to their structural manifestations in argument positions of predicates at LF is mediated by the θ-Criterion, which requires that they stand in a one-to-one correspondence:

(56) θ-Criterion
    a. Every θ-role must be assigned to just one argument chain.
    b. Every argument chain must be assigned just one θ-role.

The θ-roles characterize the argument positions of a predicate, specified as part of its lexical structure. Argument positions can differ in the semantic roles their arguments must fulfill; thus, subjects may be agents or themes, and objects may be themes, goals, patients, etc. (Jackendoff (1972)). Lexical items, such as proper names, can normally stand as arguments bearing θ-roles, and so can certain empty categories, in particular those that are $\overline{\text{A}}$-bound and function as variables. An "argument chain" is any sequence of arguments that bear occurrences of a given index. The structures in (57) are associated with degree 1 chains containing the traces as their members. It is these arguments that bear the θ-roles (here, theme) assigned to the subject positions, and not the operators that bind them:

(57)a. which agent$_2$ [e_2 is a spy]
    b. every agent$_2$ [e_2 is a spy]

Given that variables can stand as arguments of predicates, reinforcing the coincidence of the syntactic and semantic notions, we might also hold inversely, that quantified phrases do not themselves count as arguments, at least with respect to their normal interpretation via quantifi-

cation theory.[19] Then, we might speculate, on the presumption that the
θ-Criterion applies just to LF-representations, the fact that movement to
A-positions is usually reserved for phrases that are "nonreferential" (in
some sense) follows, because there is no interpretation available for such
phrases in argument positions, since they are not legitimate bearers of θ-
roles.[20] The point is more general: no phrase that is functionally an
operator can occur in an $\overline{A}$-position at LF, by the θ-Criterion, if this line of
reasoning is correct. Thus, *wh*-movement is just as much required in
nonrestrictive relative clauses, where the *wh*-phrase is effectively interpreted as a lambda-operator, as in *wh*-questions, where it is interpreted as a
(quasi)-quantifier.

In effect, then, the θ-Criterion makes LF-movement obligatory,
although the rule itself would apply optionally. Obtaining this result turns
on the assumption that quantified phrases can only be properly interpreted
as operators and are unable to bear semantic roles in argument positions.
Although to a large extent this assumption is intuitive and uncontroversial,
one need not make it. Montague (1974), for instance, does not; he allows
quantified phrases, in addition to being interpreted in operator positions,
to be interpreted in their surface positions as well. The utility of allowing
this is argued to be found in the analysis of the de dicto/de re ambiguity of
John seeks a unicorn. Leaving technical details aside, on this view *seek* is
treated as a relation between an individual and an intension, a function
from possible worlds to denotations. Assuming that *a unicorn* translates as
such a function, then the de dicto construal is just where this phrase is
interpreted as an argument of the predicate. On this interpretation, the
truth of *John seeks a unicorn* requires only that John is seeking something
with the appropriate properties, properties that in some possible world,
distinct from the actual, pick out unicorns as their extension. Thus, *John
seeks a unicorn* may be true, on this interpretation, even though John's
search is a chimerical one. The de re construal, on the other hand, is to be
represented by quantifying in, so that its truth requires that there is a
unicorn, in the actual world, and John is seeking it, an interpretation under
which it is false. One can construct accounts of this ambiguity, however,
that do not turn on assuming that *John seeks a unicorn* has any LF-
representation different from (58):

(58) a unicorn$_2$ [John seeks e_2]

Suppose, following Parsons (1980), that the domain of objects is populated
by both actual and nonactual objects. Parsons's idea is that any class of
what he calls "nuclear" properties defines a distinct object; on this view,

"being a book about linguistics" just as much characterizes an object as
"being a golden mountain" or "being a unicorn." The domain of such
objects is then further partitioned by what Parsons calls "nonnuclear"
properties, of which existence is the central case, so that our quantifiers are
existential only insofar as they are restricted to subsets of existent objects.
Now if we take verbal selection, in the sense of Chomsky (1965), to be
sensitive to this partitioning in terms of nonnuclear properties, the difference between an intensional verb like *seek* and an extensional one like
buy can be reduced to the former ambiguously selecting, for the object NP,
either positively or negatively for existence, whereas the latter only selects
positively. Thus, *John seeks a unicorn* will be false if *seek* positively selects,
since then the quantifier will range only over that subpart of the domain
containing existent objects, but true if it negatively selects, since then the
quantifiers will range over the nonexistent objects, a set that includes
unicorns. If these conjectures are on the right track, then ambiguities of
multiple quantifier scope are of a different sort from the ambiguities of
intensional transitive verbs, the former being structural, the latter not.[21]

The θ-Criterion will play other roles in ensuring that LF-representations
containing $\bar{A}$-binding properly express argument structure. For instance, it
will ensure that in multiply quantified sentences, each empty category will
correspond to a distinct variable. This is because if there is an n-tuple of
coindexed empty categories, they will form an argument chain that must be
assigned only one thematic role. This accounts for the contrast between
John$_i$ admired e$_i$ and *John$_i$ was admired e$_i$*. Each of these is associated with
the degree 2 chain $\langle John, e_i \rangle$, but it satisfies the θ-Criterion only with
respect to the latter structure. This is because in the former structure the
chain is associated with two θ-roles, those of the subject and object positions. But in the latter passive sentence, the chain is associated with but a
single θ-role, that of the object, since passive subjects are by hypothesis
dethematized (Chomsky (1981)). Turning to multiple quantification structures, since we are assuming that assignment of indices under movement is
free, distinct applications of QR can assign the same index, deriving something like (59):

(59) [every professor$_2$ [some student$_2$ [e$_2$ admires e$_2$]]]

But this violates the θ-Criterion, the relation between the empty categories
being no different from that found in improper movement structures like
Who$_2$ e$_2$ admires e$_2$. That is, the pair of traces forms a chain, and it is
associated with two θ-roles, as above. Only if the empty categories in (59)
bear different indices will each trace correspond to a distinct variable and

hence qualify as a distinct argument chain with respect to the θ-Criterion. Because the grammar thus requires that each LF-movement to an $\overline{\text{A}}$-position give rise to a distinct variable, it now follows, for instance, that *Everybody admires everybody* entails, but is not equivalent to, *Everybody admires himself*, in which the subject and object positions can be legitimately coindexed (reflexive pronouns qualifying as independent arguments for the θ-Criterion). For the same reason *Who did he admire* does not ask a reflexive question, to wit, which persons are self-admirers. This would be the interpretation if *he* and the trace of *wh* could be coindexed; but to do so would violate the θ-Criterion, for it would result once again in the illicit coindexing of thematic subject and object positions. Given the θ-Criterion, then the distinctness of variables in LF-respresentations is no isolated matter, but instead results from the same principle that accounts for improper movement and strong crossover phenomena.

In beginning this chapter, I characterized Logical Form as the level of linguistic representation interfacing the theories of linguistic form and interpretation. I have outlined one way of turning this from an operational to a formal (that is, syntactic) definition and have examined some of the basic consequences of the principles and conditions embedded in that definition. I have constructed the assumptions about the nature of the rules and representations of LF so as to extract the syntactic aspects of semantic interpretation—the "semantic structure"—and to unify it, in very basic ways, with certain "overt" aspects of syntactic structure. This reduction has been afforded in part by the hypothesis that the rules mapping onto LF share certain fundamental properties with rules mapping onto S-Structure, in particular *wh*-movement. Thus, both are movements to nonargument ($\overline{\text{A}}$-) positions, and both leave empty categories that can be structurally defined as variables; both "pied-pipe," which is important in the analysis of polarity items and VP-deletion; movement by either can derive structures that accord with the *Wh*-Criterion, give rise to crossover violations, or can be input to Absorption; and the output of each obeys general conditions on proper binding and argument structure. Just as *wh*-movement is a well-defined mapping, applying to phrases of a particular type and giving rise to a specifiable class of S-Structure representations, so too is QR, in giving rise to a definable class of LF-representations. What the commonality of these "rules" suggests is that the clusters of properties referred to as *wh*-movement and QR are reflections of deeper, more general properties of grammar; that is, both are just aspects of "Move α," their divergent properties being attributable to differential principles and conditions on S-Structure and LF. The sorts of discrepancies observed between *wh*-movement and QR—in particular, that the range of movement possibilities for LF-movement is broader than for movements onto S-Structure—indicate that movement in LF is in a sense less restricted, applying unencumbered by conditions that more severely limit the derivation of *wh*-constructions in S-Structure. LF-movements are subject only to more general conditions on LF, which are applicable as well to structures derived by S-Structure movements. The formal properties of LF-movement, then, can be thought of as the result of factoring out the conditions, universal and particular, holding just of the rules deriving, or the representations at, S-Structure.

What is left are the conditions on LF, specified ultimately by Universal Grammar, which determines the core properties of logical representations—for example, that natural language quantification is represented in operator-variable notation. To a large extent these properties of LF will be invariant from language to language, although one could imagine a range of differences as a function of independently varying properties of the S-Structure input to the rules deriving LF, for instance. Thus, we do not want to preclude the possibility that given construction types may give rise to differential classes of interpretations from language to language (although this is not to say that languages will differ in the class of propositions they can express, given the unboundedness of paraphrase). But insofar as the nature of logical representation follows from principles of Universal Grammar directly, children will need no evidence from their environment to determine its properties; these properties will be consequences of "hard-wired" aspects of the language faculty. Indeed, it is difficult to imagine what would be a sufficiently structured environment to provide evidence for a child to "learn" the various aspects of the syntax of logical form we have been considering. Plausibly, a child learning English might induce the relevant structural properties on the basis of *wh*-constructions, generalizing their formal properties to a class of semantically related elements and thus inferring that representation involving trace binding extends to the broader class of quantified sentences. The child learning English would be rather fortunate in this regard, having evidence available that a child learning Chinese, which does not have overt *wh*-movement, would not. What then would serve as evidence for the induction that quantification is represented at LF, in Chinese as well as in English, by variable binding? This suggests that the grounding of our knowledge of the logical form of language as represented at Logical Form arises from Universal Grammar and constitutes, in the final analysis, part of our innately specified knowledge of language.

Chapter 2
Government and Interpretation

The Scope Principle

When we consider the effects of assuming QR—that is, a rule that maps S-Structure onto LF, and in doing so completes the mapping from lexical argument structure, represented at D-Structure, onto logical representation—we find that it shares many (if not all) of the formal properties of "syntactic" movement rules, in particular *wh*-movement. This coincidence is sufficiently great to warrant viewing these "rules" as simply expressions of a more general rule "Move α," in the sense of Chomsky (1981). Central to the commonality between QR and *wh*-movement, when viewed from the perspective of LF, is that both give rise to structures in which a phrase in an $\bar{\text{A}}$-position—COMP for *wh*-movement and S-adjoined for QR—binds an empty category in an A-position, which can be formally defined as a "syntactic" variable and which will map directly onto the semantic notion of variable central to the interpretation of quantification. Schematically, such structures will be of the following form, where α normally will be either S or S', and β will be S:

(1) $[_\alpha \, O_i \, [_\beta \ldots e_i \ldots]]$

Now insofar as (1) represents a fundamental structural type at LF, we would expect, in accordance with our basic line of reasoning, that there are general principles of well-formedness over such structures. One such condition that has been held to apply at LF (and hence to be a condition on the output of movement operations generally, regardless of whether they map onto this level or onto S-Structure) is the Empty Category Principle (ECP): the requirement that empty categories be properly governed. As initially formulated in Chomsky (1981), the ECP has the consequence that traces in subject position can be properly governed in a language such as English only if they are "closely" bound by a phrase in an $\bar{\text{A}}$-position, such as COMP. Thus, the structure in (2) violates the ECP, because the presence of the complementizer *that* makes the coindexed trace in COMP insufficiently close to the complement subject trace, so as to disturb proper government:

(2) *$[_{S'}$ who$_2$ do you believe $[_S$ e_2 that $[_S$ e_2 suspected Philby]]]

That the ECP holds of LF was first proposed by Kayne (1981a, 1981b), who argued that aspects of the distribution of the polarity item *personne* 'no one' in French, which are apparently paradigmatic in a number of Romance languages (Rizzi (1982), Jaeggli (1980a)), follow from the ECP. *Personne* normally comes paired with the particle *ne*, and though it need not occur in the same clause with *ne*, if it does not, then according to Kayne it can only occur in object position:

(3)a. Je n'ai exigé   qu'ils   arrêtent personne.
        I neg have required that they arrest   no one
   b. *Je n'ai exigé   que personne soit arrêté.
        I neg have required that no one   be arrested

Kayne attributes this to the requirement that *personne* must be an adjunct at LF of the clause containing *ne*, to be accomplished by QR:

(4)a. personne$_2$ [je n'ai exigé qu'ils arrêtent e_2]
   b. personne$_2$ [je n'ai exigé que e_2 soit arrêté]

Although the trace is properly governed in (4a), since it is a complement to V, a lexical category, it is not in (4b), where it occurs as the complement subject, causing a violation of the ECP comparable to the *that-e* effect mentioned above.

It has been suggested by Chomsky (1981), Jaeggli (1980), and Aoun, Hornstein, and Sportiche (1981) that the ECP can be extended, in its application to LF, to "superiority" effects in multiple *wh*-constructions, so that the deviance of *What did who admire* can also be ascribed to a lack of proper government, under the assumption that *who* is moved to COMP in LF:

(5) *$[_{S'}$ who$_2$ what$_3$ $[_S$ e_2 admired e_3]]

Thus, the structural position of *what* in (5) vis-à-vis the empty category in subject position is parallel to that of *that* in (2). This contrasts with (6), the LF-representation of *Who admired what*, in which there is proper government of the subject position:

(6) $[_{S'}$ what$_3$ who$_2$ $[_S e_2$ admired $e_3]]$

Now on the analysis of May (1977), outlined in chapter 1, the multiply quantified sentence *Every student admires some professor* is assigned the following LF-representations:

(7)a. $[_{S'}[_S$ every student$_2$ $[_S$ some professor$_3$ $[_S e_2$ admires $e_3]]]]$

   b. $[_{S'}[_S$ some professor$_3$ $[_S$ every student$_2$ $[_S e_2$ admires $e_3]]]]$

These structures, derived by QR, are intended to express that the above sentence is ambiguous in a way that depends, under an appropriate interpretation, upon the scope order of the quantified phrases; they are identical, in their essentials, to those in (5) and (6). This is expected, given that LF-movements of the same type—i.e., instantiations of "Move α"—are involved in the derivation of both multiple interrogation and multiple quantification sentences. But if these are truly parallel cases, then it follows that the ECP should differentiate between (7a) and (7b), as it does between (5) and (6), with proper government of the subject position being found only in (7b). (7a) and (5) then would fall, as does (2), under the descriptive generalization that adjacency is required for a coindexed phrase in an A̅-position to govern the subject position.

Let us suppose that this generalization is correct, leaving aside until chapter 5 the exact formulation of the principles from which it may stem, and focus instead on a seemingly problematic consequence of assuming it to be so, for whatever reasons. The problem is this: Insofar as (7a) and (7b) are taken to represent the ambiguity of *Every student admires some professor*, and if (7a) is not well-formed at LF, by the ECP, then we are seemingly left without a representation in which the S-Structure subject is interpreted as having broader scope. The dilemma, then, is how this particular construal is to be represented by the grammar, given that the ECP holds of LF.

What I will suggest is that the ECP does indeed properly distinguish between structures of the basic forms illustrated in (7) and that, contrary to the views developed in May (1977), (7b) does in fact represent, from the perspective of LF, *both* scope interpretations simultaneously. More generally, I will propose that a single multiple quantified LF-representation can be seen to manifest a uniquely specifiable *class* of interpretations just in case the quantified phrases mutually c-command, or *govern*, one another. The notion "government," which will be central to the analysis, is defined as in (8), essentially following ideas due to Aoun and Sportiche (1983),

(8) α *governs* β $=_{df}$ α c-commands β and β c-commands α, and there are no maximal projection boundaries between α and β.

where c-command is defined as in (9), again following Aoun and Sportiche, the maximal categorial projections being NP, VP, AP, PP, and S′ $(= INFL^{max})$:

(9) α *c-commands* $\beta =_{df}$ every maximal projection dominating α dominates β, and α does not dominate β.

In adopting the latter definition I depart from the assumptions of chapter 1, replacing for the duration the definition of c-command drawn from Reinhart (1976), stated in terms of branching nodes.

Turning now to (10), schematically the structure of (7b), we find that both of the quantified phrases have the same c-command domain, namely S′ (S not being maximal), and hence the same (absolute) scope, given that the scope of an operator coincides with its c-command domain:

(10)

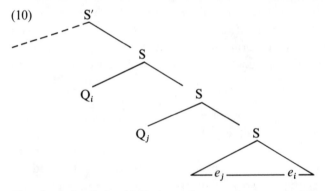

That both S-adjoined NPs have the same c-command domain entails that they c-command each other; they also satisfy the stronger structural condition, government, since there is also no maximal projection boundary intervening between them. Let us call a class of occurrences of operators Ψ a Σ-*sequence* if and only if for any O_i, $O_j \in \Psi$, O_i governs O_j, where "operator" means "phrases in $\bar{A}$-positions at LF," and let us propose that members of Σ-sequences are free to take on any type of relative scope relation. I will refer to this central assumption as the *Scope Principle*. The intent of the Scope Principle is that an LF-representation containing quantifiers forming a Σ-sequence is compatible either with there being interpretive dependencies among the member quantifiers of that sequence (in which case there will be $n!$ interpretations distinct as to relative scope for n quantifiers) or with the quantifiers being interpreted independently of one another, a type of interpretation which will include the "branching quantifiers" discussed in Hintikka (1974) and Barwise (1979). (Note that since the Scope Principle applies to *sequences*, it precludes "mixed" construals, on which some of the member quantifiers are semantically dependent, while others are independent.) By the Scope Principle, then, a quantified LF-representation associated with an n-member Σ-sequence will be compatible with $n! + 1$ interpretations, corresponding to its dependent and independent construals. As in the analysis of chapter 1, I assume that the interpretations satisfying the possibilities permissible under the Scope Principle may bear any logical relation to one another, and that they characterize the possible interpretations of a given type of syntactic structure, the preferential understandings of a sentence token being a matter falling outside the purview of the grammar per se.

Applying the Scope Principle to a concrete example, consider its application to (7b), repeated here as (11), the only LF-representation of *Every student admires some professor* consistent with the ECP:

(11) $[_{S'}[_{S}$ some professor$_3$ $[_S$ every student$_2$ $[_S$ e_2 admires $e_3]]]]$

This structure contains two quantified phrases, each with clausal (S') absolute scope, which form the Σ-sequence $\{some\ professor_3,\ every\ student_2\}$. This is because S' is the sole maximal projection dominating each of the quantified phrases, and hence the mandated structural relation, government, properly holds. In accordance with the Scope Principle, then, (11) is compatible with dependent interpretations in which either the *every*-phrase or the *some*-phrase has broader scope, as well as with an interpretation in which these phrases have no interpretive dependency. The latter, independent interpretation will be equivalent, however, to the dependent interpretation in which the *some*-phrase has broader scope, as pointed out in Hintikka (1974), although as Barwise (1979) shows, such logical equivalence will not hold for certain pairs of nonstandard quantifiers. Though I will return to the discussion of independent interpretations in chapter 4, for the most part in this chapter and in chapter 3, I will concentrate solely on dependent interpretations, given the equivalences that do hold with standard quantifiers.

In those structures in which the Scope Principle is not satisfied—that is, when an LF-representation contains quantifiers that do not govern one another—the grammar will make available only a dependent interpretation, relative scope order being fixed simply as a function of constituency, determined in a "top-to-bottom" fashion, from structurally superior to structurally inferior phrases. For instance, in *Everyone believes that someone is a spy*, with a de dicto interpretation, the *every*-phrase will be adjoined to the matrix clause and the *some*-phrase to the complement. Since in these positions the quantified phrases do not govern one another, the only interpretation will be one in which the former phrase has broader scope over the latter. In all other cases, where there is no structural relation, the quantifiers are interpreted independently; a trivial consequence is that there will be no scope dependencies between quantifiers in distinct sentences.

One immediate advantage of the approach I am advocating here is that the structural relations we now find among clusters of $\bar{\text{A}}$-adjoined quantified phrases will be sufficient to allow interpretation via the binary quantifications developed in Higginbotham and May (1981a) and discussed in chapter 1. Recall that this type of derived quantifier interpretation was argued to apply only for mutually c-commanding quantifier phrases, and, since the "branching node" definition of c-command was assumed, it was maintained that such configurations arose through Absorption, which structurally readjusted the output of QR. Once Absorption applied, both pronouns in *Every pilot who shot at it hit some MIG that chased him*, for instance, would then qualify as bound variables. But this symmetry of c-command is now found directly represented in the LF-representation of such sentences, which structurally will be of the same form as (10). Therefore, there need be no recourse to an actual rule of "Absorption."

Holding that a single structure at LF represents a class of interpretations differs in an important way from the analysis presented in Chapter 1, essentially that of May (1977), in that multiply quantified sentences are no longer disambiguated with respect to their LF-representations, but rather with respect to the interpretations with which their LF-representations are compatible. The Scope Principle determines this compatibility, linking LF-representations within the syntactic component and their interpretations within the semantic component. LF-representations syntactically encode "instructions" (to use Kempson's (1983) felicitous term) for semantic interpretation, which the Scope Principle deciphers in terms of the permissible orders in which quantifications can apply to such structures so as to determine their truth-conditions. Alternatively, it might be assumed that LF is indirectly interpreted, structures at this level being associated with a set of logical "translations," each expressing a distinct way in which the constituents of a well-formed LF-representation may be compositionally related. Such logical translations would be, to a large extent, simply reflexes of the LF-representation from which they are projected, being constrained to preserve those aspects of function-argument, scope, and binding relations that are represented in terms of configurational constituency at LF. It would be to such representations that interpretations are assigned, the Scope Principle being thought of as a rule for the projection of logical translations from LF. (The distinction I am drawing between direct and indirect interpretation harks back to that between Montague's "English as a Formal Language" and "PTQ" systems, although without necessarily accepting Montague's syntactic or semantic assumptions; see Montague (1974).) A version of the latter sort of view is eloquently developed by Ladusaw (1983),[1] who points out that there may very well be an empirical issue lurking between these approaches, in that logical translations need not preserve the constituent structure of the LF-representations, since the form in which they represent compositional structure will be, in large part, a function of the particular assumptions made about the way "meanings" of constituents are to be expressed and combined. Thus, if we find that establishing the proper conditions on interpretation requires reference to aspects of the structure of *meanings*, distinct from the syntax of LF, then this would constitute evidence for an indirect system of interpretation via logical translations. Partee and Bach (1984) attempt to construct such an argument on the basis of VP-deletion constructions; they argue that an account of the identity conditions in this construction involves mentioning binding into verb phrase translations. My purpose here, however, is not to join the issue over direct versus indirect interpretation, but rather only to draw out the possible significance of the distinction and to establish that it is LF that is the level of natural language *syntactic* representation that is the input to the semantics, regardless of which particular view of interpretation one ultimately assumes.

As a final point it should be kept in mind that the interpretive freedom allowed under the Scope Principle does not undermine the claim that movement is involved in the derivation of LF-representations of quantified sentences. Indeed, only if there *is* movement could there be structures in which the Scope Principle is satisfied, in general. What is immaterial for scope, on this view, is the relative structural positions of the phrases falling under this principle; thus, (7a), if well-formed, would express the same range of interpretations as (7b). Relative position *is* of importance, however, with respect to the ECP, and this is what rules out (7a). Thus, our initial motivation for maintaining that multiple quantification sentences have a single LF-representation is syntactic—it is a consequence of a structural well-formedness condition, which in part characterizes LF.[2]

Wh-Phrases and Quantifier Phrases: Syntax

Clearly, a grammar that assumes the general application of the ECP and the Scope Principle will be extensionally equivalent, at least with respect to the cases considered thus far, to a grammar that simply stipulates that the

ECP is not relevant, for whatever reasons, to representations like those in (7). In such a grammar it would not be necessary to assume the Scope Principle. There is evidence, however, indicating the correctness of an approach that does. Thus, consider (12), which illustrates an interesting interaction between *wh*-phrases and universal quantifiers:[3]

(12) What did everyone buy for Max?

A question like (12) displays an ambiguity; it may be understood, loosely, either as a single question, asking for the identity of the object such that everyone bought it for Max, or as a "distributed" question, asking of each individual what it is that that person bought for Max. On the former construal (13a) is an appropriate answer; on the latter, (13b). I return to the relevant semantics in the next section.

(13)a. Everyone bought Max a Bosendorfer piano.
   b. Mary bought Max a tie, Sally a sweater, and Harry a piano.

(14) is the LF-representation of (12); it differs from the S-Structure representation of (12) only in that via LF-movement the subject NP has been adjoined to S, a position from which it properly governs its trace. The trace of the *wh*-phrase in COMP is properly governed by the verb:

(14) $[_{S'}$ what$_2$ $[_S$ everyone$_3$ $[_S$ e_3 bought e_2 for Max$]]]$

Taking *wh*-phrases in interrogatives as scopal elements, if it is assumed that scope is solely a function of relative structural position, as in the treatment described in chapter 1, then we would expect (14) to represent only an interpretation in which the *wh*-phrase has broader scope, that is, the first construal described above to which (13a) is an appropriate answer.[4] On the other hand, if we assume the Scope Principle, then it follows that (12) is ambiguous with respect to the relative scopes of *what* and *everyone*, which c-command each other, and hence govern (since S' is the sole maximal projection dominating each phrase, and, as with cases like (7b), only an S bracket, the boundary of a nonmaximal projection, intervenes between them). Therefore, (14) represents the second construal, as well as the first, exhibiting just the range of interpretations allowed, as a function of scope, by the Scope Principle.

This quantifier-*wh* ambiguity is not restricted to the simple type of cases considered thus far. It is also found, for instance, in cases of "long" *wh*-movement from an embedded clause, as in (15),

(15) Who did everyone say admired Bill/Bill admired?

or when the *wh*-phrase is adverbial, as in *Where did everyone go for their summer vacation* or *When did everyone see Max*. Nor is it necessary for the quantified phrase to occur in the subject position to give rise to the ambiguity; compare *When did Max see everyone* to the last cited example, or dative sentences like *What did you buy (for) everyone*.[5] The common thread in the analysis of all these sentences is that in their LF-representations, as in (14), the *every*-phrase can be moved to the S-adjoined position, where it can be interpreted as interacting freely in terms of scope with the *wh*-phrase in COMP.

Primary to the motivation for the Scope Principle is its interaction with the ECP, and the intimate relation of these principles can be further seen by considering (16), whose D-Structure representation is parallel to that of (12), but in which the subject, rather than the object, NP has been moved to COMP at S-Structure:

(16) Who bought everything for Max?

The ambiguity of (12) starkly contrasts with the nonambiguity of (16), which has only the interpretation as a single collective question. Thus, only (17) is an appropriate answer to (16):

(17) Oscar bought everything for Max.

Notice that (13b), *Mary bought Max a tie, Sally a sweater, and Harry a piano*, is not an appropriate answer to (16), from which it can be concluded that (16) does not express a distributed question of the sort associated with (12). Examples like (12) and (16) thus exhibit a subject-object asymmetry, turning on whether a subject or an object *wh*-phrase has been moved to COMP.

This asymmetry is found as well in pairs like (18a) and (18b), with stress on *Dickens* in both cases, so as to abstract away from the effects of focus:[6]

(18)a. Which of Dickens's books has each of you read?
     b. Which of you has read each of Dickens's books?

Though (18a) allows an interpretation permitting answers such as "Max has read *Oliver Twist*, Ken has read *Bleak House*, and Oscar has read *David Copperfield*," this is not an appropriate answer to (18b). Rather, (18b) can only be understood as a request for the identity of that individual who has read Dickens's *oeuvre*. A similar case is mentioned in Karttunen and Peters (1980, 197–198):[7]

(19)a. Which customer is each clerk now serving?
     b. Which clerk is now serving each customer?

Karttunen and Peters evaluate (20) as an answer to these questions with respect to a situation depicting a supermarket checkout area, in which there are three clerks (call them John, Max, and Oscar) and a number of customers lined up at each of their checkout counters (assuming a one-to-one relationship between clerks and customers):

(20) John is serving customer D, Max is serving customer H, and Oscar is serving customer L.

Karttunen and Peters observe that (20) is "unobjectionable" as an answer to (19a), but that there is "something wrong" about using it as an answer to (19b). As above, these distinctions follow from the assumption that a quantified phrase can have broader scope than a *wh*-phrase in COMP only if it occurs in the subject position. That (18a) and (19a) allow wide scope for the quantified phrase (in addition to narrow scope) might not be surprising, given the frequently made assumption that *each* is a "wide scope" quantifier. But then what is surprising is that their (b) counterparts apparently *lack* broad scope construals for the *each*-phrases. Thus, it seems that the ambiguity under discussion, or lack thereof, is a structural fact of LF, to a large extent independent of inherent properties of the various quantifiers having universal import.

Sentences such as *Who did they see at the Wimbledon finals*, containing plural pronouns, also display the ambiguity that interests us here, as pointed out by Haïk (1984). Thus, it can be construed as a question asking, for the members of some (contextually fixed) group, who each one saw. This is again not surprising, since plural NPs often act as quantified phrases, interacting in terms of scope with other quantified phrases; thus, no comparable ambiguity is to be found upon substitution of a singular pronoun. The minimally contrasting *Who saw them at the Wimbledon finals*, on the other hand, does not display the ambiguity in question; again, only the *wh*-phrase can have broad scope. But although it is difficult here to distinguish a purportedly quantificational use of the plural NP from its use as a simple, referring pronominal phrase, it is important that the latter example does not display the ambiguity of the former. Finally, other quantificational elements also display the same sort of subject-object asymmetry with regard to scope. For instance, note the ambiguity of the numerical sentence *Which professor do those two students admire* in contrast with the singulary interpretation of *Which student admires those two professors*,[8] or the contrast between *Tell me what some/many of your students are writing dissertations on* and *Tell me who are writing dissertations on some/many of the central issues in linguistics*. In the latter contrast either question can be answered by specifying the value of the *wh*-phrase; the first one by fixing the topics, the second by fixing the students. But only the former example, it would appear, admits answers pairing issues and students such as *Jones is writing on island constraints, Smith on pro-drop, and Doe on backwards anaphora* (presuming that Jones, Smith, and Doe constitute some/many of the students).

What, then, is the reason for this discrepancy in interpretation, of which such a closely related pair as (12) and (16) is an exemplar? If the *wh*- and quantified phrases were simply allowed to vary freely in relative scope, then we would expect to find that both (12) and (16) were ambiguous.[9] But this is not the case; rather, there is a clear asymmetry depending upon whether *wh*-movement has been from subject or object position. Interestingly, this is just the difference that the superiority facts discussed in the previous section turned on; recall the discussion of (5) and (6). The issue, then, is this: Why is it possible to "quantify in" to a question—so as to give the distributive construal—when *wh*-movement has been from object position, but not when it has been from subject position? In the latter circumstance, the scope of the quantified phrase must be contained within the scope of *wh*, thus allowing only for a construal as a collective question.

We have already answered half of this question: quantifying *into* a question is possible just when a structure can be derived at LF that satisfies the Scope Principle. We have seen this to be so in (14). But now consider (21), the LF-representation of (16), derived (as is (14)) by adjunction of the quantified phrase to S:

(14) $[_{s'}$ what$_2$ $[_s$ everyone$_3$ $[_s$ e_3 bought e_2 for Max]]]

(21) $[_{s'}$ who$_3$ $[_s$ everything$_2$ $[_s$ e_3 bought e_2 for Max]]]

(21), in contrast to (14), violates the ECP. This is because the subject empty category is not properly governed, the presence of the intervening S-adjoined phrase serving to block this (just as in (7a)). Thus, an LF-representation under which (16) would be construed as ambiguous is not derived. But this raises a problem. What *is* the LF-representation of (16)? After all, the claim is only that it is unambiguous, not that it is ungrammatical.

In deriving (14) and (21) we assumed that LF-movement is to S, comparable to the restriction that movement of *wh*-phrases must be solely to COMP. It is not clear, however, that LF-movements should be limited in this fashion; that is, we may wish to assume that they (in some sense to be made concrete) more closely approximate "Move α" than S-Structure movements. That is, insofar as grammars idiosyncratically limit movement operations, we would typically expect S-Structure to be the locus of such marked properties of rules. This is because it is representations at this level that are subject to phonological interpretation as phonetic strings and hence could serve, in principle, as evidence overtly available to the child acquiring a grammar. It is unclear, however, just what might serve as comparable evidence for idiosyncratic properties of movements onto LF (aside from indirect evidence garnered from properties of S-Structure); thus, everything else being equal, we would expect LF to exhibit derivational possibilities of a more general nature than those found at S-Structure. One way we might take LF-movement as more closely approximating "More α," then, is by assuming that it is not limited to adjoining to S, but rather has freer possibilities of adjunction. In particular, this would allow QR to attach a phrase to nodes other than S, so long as such movements were consistent with proper binding, the θ-Criterion, the ECP, etc. In the case at hand, this means that from the S-Structure representation of (16), QR can derive another structure besides (21), in which the S-Structure object is adjoined to VP rather than to S. That such movements should be permitted has been suggested by Williams (1977) in his discussion of VP-deletion. It will derive for (16) the LF-representation in (22):

(22) $[_{S'}$ who$_3$ $[_S$ e_3 $[_{VP}$ everything$_2$ $[_{VP}$ bought e_2' for Max]]]]

(22) satisfies the ECP: *everything* no longer intrudes between the *wh*-phrase and its trace, and, as before, the trace of *everything* is properly bound by a phrase in an $\overline{\text{A}}$-position (hence qualifying as a variable) and satisfies the ECP (again being properly governed by V). Moreover, (22) does not satisfy the Scope Principle, since a maximal projection boundary, that of VP, intervenes between the *wh*-phrase and the quantified phrase (recall that it is the outermost brackets that constitute a projection boundary). In that case, the default procedure for scope determination is applicable; that is, scope is simply a function of hierarchical constituent structure. Thus, the *wh*-phrase must be interpreted as having broader scope. This correctly accounts for the nonambiguity of (16), as opposed to (12), primarily as a function of the ECP, which allows only (22) as the LF-representation of (16).[10]

There are independent arguments supporting the claim that the LF-representations of sentences like (16) involve adjunction to VP. Williams (1977) notes the ambiguity of (23), among other cases, and attributes it to whether the quantified phrase is adjoined to VP (collective) or to S (distributed):

(23) Max saw everyone before Bill did.

This difference in adjunction will correlate with whether the quantified phrase, or just the variable it binds, is "reconstructed" back into the position of the missing VP. Now note that (23) contrasts with (24):

(24) Who saw everyone before Bill did?

(24) appears to have only the "collective" construal; the "distributed" construal also found in (23) is lacking. This follows immediately from the impossibility of S-adjunction in the presence of a phrase in COMP; hence, the only LF-representation for (24) is one in which *everyone* is adjoined to VP. In contrast, since (23) contains no *wh*-phrase that would cause an ECP violation, S-adjunction is possible there, giving the added construal.

   Another piece of evidence, although considerably more subtle, is found in the contrast of pairs like the following:

(25)a. Which of his poems did every poet read?
    b. Which of his poems were read by every poet?

In (25a) the pronoun *his* can apparently be understood as bound by *every poet*; see Engdahl (1980), where many of the problems attending these sorts of examples are considered. In contrast, anaphora seems considerably less possible in (25b); the pronoun is most naturally understood as designating an individual distinct from those falling within the (contextually determined) domain satisfying the quantification interpreting the *every*-phrase. This is explicable on the assumptions made here, since only the LF-representation of (25a) will satisfy the Scope Principle, and it is here that anaphora is possible. But in the LF-representation of (25b) the Scope Principle is not satisfied; rather, *every poet* will be adjoined to VP and hence cannot be interpreted as having the *wh*-phrase containing the pronoun within its scope. In this case bound variable anaphora is excluded.[11]

   Also bearing on the issue are examples like (26), in which a quantified phrase stands as the subject of an infinitival complement to *expect*, an "exceptional Case-marking" environment:

(26) What kind of sales do you expect each of Heller's books to achieve?

As with cases involving a quantified phrase in object position, (26) is ambiguous. Either the *wh*-phrase can be construed with broader scope, in which case *Record sales!* would be an appropriate answer, or it can be construed with narrower scope, in which case (27) would:

(27) Record sales for *Catch 22*, mediocre for *Good as Gold*, and lousy for *Something Happened*.

The following example supports the view that LF-movement is possible from the governed complement subject position of exceptional Case-marking verbs like *expect* and *believe*:

(28) Dulles believed no agent to be competent to discover moles before Angleton did.

The most natural interpretation of this sentence asserts that Angleton came to have a class of de re beliefs before Dulles. This is accounted for if the quantified phrase has broad scope, so that the representation of this sentence after the deleted VP has been reconstructed is loosely as shown in (29):

(29) [no agent$_2$ [Dulles believed [e_2 to be competent to discover moles]] [before Angleton believed [e_2 to be competent to discover moles]]]

It is clear that this represents the intended interpretation; note that both of the empty categories in this structure satisfy the ECP.

Now assuming that LF-movement can extract from such complement subject positions, the LF-representation of (26) will be (30):

(30) [$_{S'}$ what kind of sales$_2$ [$_S$ each of Heller's books$_3$ [$_S$ you expect [e_3 to achieve e_2]]]]

(30) satisfies the Scope Principle; as in (14), the *wh*-phrase and the quantified phrase are in the structural relation—government—under which free relative scope ordering is possible. This is expected. But now consider (31):

(31) Which of you expects each of Heller's books to achieve record sales?

Here the possibilities of interpretation are markedly different from those found in (26). This sentence is unambiguous, possessing only an interpretation in which the *wh*-phrase has broader scope; that is, it can only be taken as an inquiry into the identity of an individual holding a particular expectation with respect to book sales. It does not have a construal in which the quantified phrase has broader scope than the *wh*-phrase, even though the quantifier is *each* (a quantifier prone to wide scope interpretation) and occurs in an S-Structure position from which, in the closely related (26), extraction to the broad scope position is possible. Notice finally that the quantified phrase takes narrow scope with respect to the *wh*-phrase in

COMP regardless of whether it is understood as standing inside or outside the scope of the matrix predicate.

Where the structure of (31) differs from that of (26) is that in the former *wh*-movement is from the matrix subject, whereas in the latter it is from a complement object position. Thus, if LF-movement were to extract the quantified phrase and adjoin it to S, as in (30), the result would be (32):

(32) *[$_{S'}$ which of you$_2$ [$_S$ each of Heller's books$_3$ [$_S$ e_2 expects [e_3 to achieve record sales]]]]

But (32) is not well-formed. Just like (21), it violates the ECP, the matrix subject trace not being properly governed. But again there is an alternative, namely that QR can adjoin the quantified phrase to VP:

(33) [$_{S'}$ which of you$_2$ [$_S$ e_2 [$_{VP}$ each of Heller's books$_3$ [$_{VP}$ expects [e_3 to achieve record sales]]]]]

The ECP is satisfied in (33), as in (22). And, again as in (22), the scope order in this structure is fixed, the *wh*-phrase being required to have broader scope. This accurately characterizes just that more limited range of interpretation expressed by (31), in opposition to the minimally contrasting (26).[12]

The nonambiguity of (31) contrasts with the ambiguity of (34), which has the same structure but contains two quantifiers:

(34) Everyone expects someone to be a spy.

This is because each of the quantified phrases in (34) can be attached to S in a way that allows for proper government of the matrix subject position:

(35) [someone$_3$ [everyone$_2$ [e_2 expects [e_3 to be a spy]]]]

Thus, the difference between (31) and (35) turns on the facts that the *wh*-phrase in the former attains its position in the mapping to S-Structure, and that that position is fixed in the further mapping onto LF. But for multiple quantifiers there is greater freedom in deriving the latter level, and this accounts for the greater range of interpretation found in (35).

A contrast comparable to the one between (26) and (31) is found in (36a) and (36b); (36a) exhibits the now familiar ambiguity of scope, whereas (36b) has only an interpretation under which the *wh*-phrase has broader scope:

(36)a. Who do you think everyone saw at the rally?
  b. Who thinks everyone saw you at the rally?

The analysis of these examples proceeds along precisely the same lines as that of (26) and (31). Presuming that *everyone* can be extracted from the complement to the matrix clause in (36a) will allow it to govern, and be governed by, the *wh*-phrase in COMP, with which it can therefore freely vary in scope. In (36b), on the other hand, such extraction would only move the quantified phrase to a position in which it would block proper government of the trace of the *wh*-phrase in the matrix subject position. A well-formed LF-representation is possible, therefore, only if *everyone* in this sentence is adjoined in some lower position, a position in which it will be required to have scope narrower than *who*. The same contrast in interpretation arises if *that* is added to the examples in (36); thus, *Who do you think that everyone saw at the rally* is ambiguous and *Who thinks that everyone saw you at the rally* is unambiguous. I will return to this, and its importance for the ECP, in chapter 5.

Although the ambiguity of (36a) sufficiently argues for the possibility of QR extracting phrases from tensed complement domains to the matrix, it is interesting to note the contrast between (37) and (28), the example that was used to motivate the possibility of extraction from the subjects of infinitival complements of verbs like *believe*:

(37) Dulles believed no agent was competent to discover moles before Angleton did.

Though an interpretation parallel to that of (28) is perhaps not impossible here, the more natural construal of (37) is that Dulles had a belief de dicto before Angleton. Though it is not altogether clear why this should be, the reason is no doubt related to the fact that the subject of an infinitival complement to *believe* is directly governed by that predicate, but not the subject of a finite complement. This may be likened to Quine's (1955) notion of "exportation" in the analysis of semantic transparency, in which an argument of the complement to *believe* is, so to speak, reanalyzed, to become an argument of the higher predicate. In the syntax of exceptional Case-marking predicates, we might conjecture, this is directly represented in its syntax, with respect to the complement subject position.

Finally, the same sort of contrast in interpretation that we have seen between *wh*-phrases and quantifier phrases shows itself in *wh*-constructions other than questions, as can be seen in the free relatives in (38):

(38)a. Whichever student every professor admires will graduate.
    b. Whichever student admires every professor will graduate.

Thus, (38a) allows a broad scope, in addition to a narrow scope, construal for the *every*-phrase; (38b) allows only the latter. The explanation at this point should be clear: only in the former sentence will adjunction to S be consistent with the ECP, and only adjunction to this position will give rise to the possibility of a broad scope interpretation under the Scope Principle.[13] The existence of the asymmetry of interpretation in free relatives shows, then, that whatever account is to be proposed of this phenomenon cannot turn solely on the properties, syntactic or semantic, of questions per se, but must depend on the properties that questions share with other *wh*-constructions.

Wh-Phrases and Quantifier Phrases: Semantics

In this section I turn to some semantic issues in the analysis of the sort of universally distributed questions under consideration in this chapter, before returning, in the next chapter, to primarily syntactic concerns.

Suppose, following Higginbotham and May (1981a), that the *question* interpreting an LF-representation of a *wh*-question consists of a set of *theories*, assignments of truth-values to pairs $(\psi(x), a)$, for each $a \in D$, D a subset of the universe of individuals U. An *answer* to a question $\mathbf{Q}$ is a sentence that is incompatible with at least one theory in $\mathbf{Q}$. Thus, the LF-representation of *Which men left*, namely (39),

(39) $[_{S'} \text{ which men}_2 \, [_S \, e_2 \, \text{left}]]$

will be interpreted by the question $\mathbf{Q}$, consisting of assignments of truth-values to pairs of the form $(x \text{ left}, a)$, for $a \in D$, D being the set of men. I presume that *wh*-phrases pick out restricted domains, as do other natural language quantifiers. *John left* will then be an answer to (39), because its truth is logically inconsistent with the theory that assigns falsehood to the pair $(x \text{ left}, John)$. An answer is *complete* if and only if it is incompatible with all but one theory in $\mathbf{Q}$; *partial* otherwise. LF-representations of *wh*-questions, then, express (or designate) questions, that is, sets of theories that determine which sentences qualify as answers. They do not, strictly speaking, designate their (true) answers (or more precisely, the propositions that express them), as in other approaches (Karttunen (1977)).

(40) is the LF-representation associated with the question *Who did everyone see*:

(40) $[_{S'} \text{ who}_2 \, [_S \, \text{everyone}_3 \, [_S \, e_3 \, \text{saw} \, e_2]]]$

As established above, (40) can be interpreted with the quantifiers in either scope order. If it is taken with the *wh*-phrase having broader scope, it expresses the question consisting of assignments of truth-values to pairs of the form (*everyone saw x, a*), for $a \in D$. Thus, *Everyone saw John* is an answer, on the construal under discussion, since it is logically inconsistent with the theory assigning falsehood to (*everyone saw x, John*). It will be a complete answer if and only if $D = \{John\}$, where this is fixed by pragmatic considerations falling outside the grammar proper. It is a partial answer if the cardinality of D is greater than one.

Now consider the interpretation assigned to (40) when *everyone* has broader scope. Suppose there is a subset D' of U. The question expressed by (40) will then correspond to assignments of truth-values to pairs of the form (*b saw x, a*), $a \in D$, for each $b \in D'$. That is, associated with each member of D' is a set of theories **Q**. We may think of the question associated with (40) on this construal as the set of sets of theories **Q** associated with each member of D'. Call this **Q***. Answers to **Q*** must be exhaustive, in that they must provide an answer for each $Q \in Q^*$. Answers for each **Q**, however, may be partial or complete, in the sense described above.

Thus, (41) and (42) are answers to *Who did everyone see*, with *everyone* having broad scope; they are exhaustive if $D' = \{Mary, Sally, Carol\}$:

(41) Mary saw John, Sally saw Bill, and Carol saw Jones.

(42)a. Mary saw Carol, Sally saw Mary, and Carol saw Sally.
   b. Mary, Carol, and Sally each saw themselves.

Although (41) and (42) count as possible answers, simply in being exhaustive, they are not appropriate in all the same circumstances; this varies as a function of the relation of D and D'. Thus, if D and D' have no members in common, (41) is an answer, but not (42), the latter not being incompatible with any theory in the question. On the other hand, if $D = D'$, the situation is reversed; then (41) is not incompatible with any theory, and it is only (42a–b) that count as legitimate answers.

R. Kempson points out that the *every*-phrase in *She told me who inspected every school* can have broader scope than the *wh*-phrase, in contrast to the simplex *Who inspected every school*. While this is so, notice further that the quantifier is also understood as having scope broader than the matrix predicate, and lacks an indirect "family of questions" interpretation. This absence results because the extension from **Q** to **Q*** is defined recursively with respect to assignments to the variables in a given open sentence, and thus is to be found only when a quantifier contains a *wh*-phrase immediately within its scope because both are members of a single

Σ-sequence. In contrast to the above example, then, is *John told me which school everybody inspected*, which admits the family of questions construal, but not one in which the quantifier has maximally broad scope, a consequence, I presume, of the ECP restricting LF-movement from the complement subject position.

What is expressed by the LF-representations of *wh*-questions, then, are questions, in the formal sense. The construals of (40) differ in that one "asks" a single question, the other a composite question. It is perfectly consistent with our semantics that each of the subquestions under the latter construal may have distinct (partial or complete) answers, since strictly speaking, a question is asked for each individual denoted by the universally quantified phrase. Moreover, each of the distinct questions within Q^* will carry over its presuppositions, if any. In particular, if the LF-representations of *wh*-questions express questions, in the formal sense, then the presupposition of singular *wh*-phrases amounts to the stricture that the free variable in each theory in Q is satisfied by a single member of D. When Q is extended to Q^*, the presupposition remains for each Q in Q^*, although nothing restricts the satisfier of each member Q of Q^* to the same member of D. On this view, the singular presupposition found in questions with singular *wh*-phrases limits what constitutes an answer by placing constraints on the semantic structure of questions. It only indirectly restricts the cardinality of the set of answers, which is also a function of the size of D'. In this regard, Hirschbühler (1978, 16–23) points out the importance of viewing singular *wh*-questions under this construal as involving families of questions, since otherwise the interpretations assigned to *Which book did every professor assign* will be equivalent, regardless of the scope order of the *wh*- and quantifier phrases.

In his analysis of questions, Karttunen (1977) also discusses the sort of examples we have been considering in this section. Karttunen's proposal is that *wh*-questions designate the set of propositions expressing their true answers, which he embeds formally in the context of the syntax and semantics of Montague grammar. Since Karttunen's approach individuates questions on the basis of their propositional content, it suffers from the flaw, pointed out in Higginbotham and May (1981a), that it identifies two questions if they designate necessarily equivalent propositions. Consequently, *What is the sum of 16 and 2* will express, in Karttunen's approach, the same question as *What is the product of 3 and 6*. Putting this rather significant defect aside, however, consider Karttunen's treatment of sentences like *What did everyone buy for Max*, whose ambiguity he seeks to reduce to the ambiguity of the indirect question (43):

(43) John knows what everyone bought for Max.

In Karttunen's syntax, quantifiers, including *wh*-phrases, may be "quantified in" only on S. But whereas the output of this rule is also an S for non-
wh-phrases, it is of category Q, distinct from S, for *wh*-phrases.[14] Consequently, *everyone* can be quantified in either at the matrix clause or at the
embedded clause in deriving (43), but in the latter case it must have scope
narrower than *what*, since otherwise the quantification rule would have
illicitly taken a complement of category Q as its argument. (However,
existence of a "broad scope" interpretation as evidence for this analysis is
somewhat vitiated by the observation that when *know* is understood extensionally the interpretation in which the quantifier has broad scope over
both the *wh*-phrase and the matrix predicate is equivalent to the interpretation in which it has scope only over the *wh*-phrase. See Groenendijk and
Stokhof (1982).) Karttunen extends the analysis to direct questions by
assuming that they are covertly within the scope of a performative
operator. Then the quantifier phrase can be seen as taking scope with
respect to it, just as it does with respect to *know* in the analysis of (43). Of
course, this assumes that the problems of a performative analysis can be
adequately worked out; see Hirschbühler (1978) for an attempt. But even
so, it is unclear how the analysis would be able to block a broad scope
interpretation for the quantified phrase in *Who bought everything for Max*.

    Karttunen and Peters (1980) modify the analysis of quantifier-*wh* inter-
actions so as to allow directly for quantifying into questions. As discussed
above, they recognize that there is a distinction between (19a) and (19b),
which I have argued to be an instance of a much more general
phenomenon:

(19)a. Which customer is each clerk now serving?
    b. Which clerk is now serving each customer?

They maintain that only the former question is consistent with the
enumerative answer in (20):

(20) John is serving customer D, Max is serving customer H, and Oscar
      is serving customer L.

On the view taken here this is because only (19a) can be associated with an
LF-representation in which the object quantified phrase has broader scope,
and which is thus assigned a "family of questions" interpretation. One
would expect Karttunen and Peters to make a similar distinction; they
adopt Karttunen's analysis that questions denote those propositions that

express their true answers, leading one to suppose that (19a) and (19b) are interpretively distinct. But Karttunen and Peters explicitly deny this, maintaining, somewhat paradoxically, that these examples "do not ... express different questions—whatever is the correct answer to one will also be the correct answer to the [other]." The reason for this is that the syntactic construction they assume cannot be so constrained that it assigns different questions to (19a) and (19b); as stated, it is possible to quantify into either the subject or object position of a question. What they do argue is that the difference arises from these two questions being associated with distinct conversational implicatures, which makes only (19a) appropriate in the circumstance described above. That is, since the clerk-to-customer relationship in a supermarket is usually one-to-one, it would be odd to use a question like (19b) that presumably presupposes that it is one-to-many, implicating, in Karttunen and Peters's words, "... that all customers are being served by some clerk..." True enough, but since Karttunen and Peters claim that both examples in (19) denote the same questions, there should be a reading of (19a) in which it also has this implicature, and a reading of (19b) in which it does not so that either should be equally natural (or unnatural); but this is contrary to Karttunen and Peters's claim. Unfortunately, since Karttunen and Peters provide no explicit formulation of implicature, it is impossible to determine why it should be that the relevant presupposition is present only when the universally quantified phrase occurs in object position, but not when it occurs in the subject. Of course, one very salient hypothesis presents itself: namely, that this phenomenon occurs because (19a) and (19b) are associated with different classes of interpretation, the former being ambiguous and the latter unambiguous. But this is precisely the hypothesis we have been entertaining in this chapter.

The problem with the line of analysis in Karttunen (1977) and Karttunen and Peters (1980) is one it shares with virtually all other discussions of quantifier-*wh* scope interactions (see the references cited in note 3). Just those mechanisms developed to account for the ambiguity found with *wh*-movement from object position will also allow for the attribution of an exactly parallel ambiguity when the *wh*-phrase is displaced from subject position. However, the problem is not strictly speaking semantic, but rather syntactic. The semantics sketched above would err in just the same way were it not wedded to an appropriately constrained syntax; the failure of *Who bought everything for Max*, for instance, to express what is otherwise a semantically possible construal arises from constraints on "logical syntax"—concretely, the Empty Category Principle as it interacts with the Scope Principle at the level of Logical Form. And insofar as such syntactic constraints limit well-formedness at this level, the logical form of natural language will depart from that of a "logically perfect" language, in that there will be semantically composable meanings that have no direct syntactic expression.

Chapter 3
Nodes and Projections

The Structure of Adjunction

In this chapter I return to issues that arose in the context of assumptions regarding the syntax of LF-representations. In particular, I want to consider the claim brought out in chapter 2 that LF-movement amounts to applying "Move α" in the mapping onto LF, and hence that it can apply quite generally in adjoining to various syntactic positions.[1] In the context of quantifier-*wh* scope interactions we saw that VP, as well as S, is among the positions to which quantified phrases can be legitimately adjoined at LF. Perhaps the most well-know argument to this conclusion arises in the context of VP-deletion; as Sag (1976) and Williams (1977) discuss, sentences like *Some student admires every professor* are ambiguous in isolation, but in a VP-deletion context, as in (1), the ambiguity evaporates, and only a specific construal is available.[2]

(1) Some student admires every professor, but John doesn't.

The reason for this, following essentially the particulars of Williams's approach, is that only reconstructing a VP that contains the *every*-phrase will give rise to a well-formed logical representation, a circumstance that will not obtain if this phrase has broader scope. The relevant structures are (2a–b):

(2)a. [$_S$ some student$_2$ [$_S$ e_2 [$_{VP}$ every professor$_3$ [$_{VP}$ admires e_3]]]], but John doesn't [$_{VP}$every professor$_3$ [$_{VP}$ admire e_3]]

   b. [$_S$ every professor$_3$ [$_S$ some student$_2$ [$_S$ e_2 [$_{VP}$ admires e_3]]]], but John doesn't [$_{VP}$ admire e_3]

The problem with (2b) is that the second conjunct contains a free variable, since the scope of *every professor* is limited to the initial conjunct. No such problem arises in (2a), however; since the VP-adjoined phrase is reconstructed along with the rest of VP, all variables occuring in this conjunct are properly bound. But, as we have seen, quantified phrases adjoined in this position are required to take narrower scope than S-adjoined phrases; this accounts for the univocal interpretation of (1).[3]

A further argument for LF-movement to VP is to be found in the context of weak crossover. One approach to this phenomenon, the Bijection Principle, initially broached in Koopman and Sportiche (1982), requires a one-to-one relation between operators and $\bar{\text{A}}$-bound phrases. Weak crossover examples like *Who does his mother admire* are then ruled out because the *wh*-phrase, under the relevant interpretation, directly binds both the pronoun and its trace. This analysis extends to examples like *His mother admires everyone*, given that, at LF, its structure is identical, in the relevant respects, to that of the *wh*-question. Safir (1984) explores an extension of this basic approach. He points out that the Bijection Principle is incorrect as it stands, since it rules out parasitic gap constructions, such as *Which article did you read e without filing e*, and across-the-board constructions, such as *Who does Sally despise e and Sam admire e*, in which there is multiple $\bar{\text{A}}$-binding by a single operator. Safir proposes that a single operator can $\bar{\text{A}}$-bind multiple variables, but only up to parallelism; that is, all of the bound categories must be of the same syntactic type. Weak crossover violates this latter constraint, since one bound category is a pronoun and the other an empty category, but no such mismatch is found in parasitic gap or across-the-board constructions, where only empty categories are $\bar{\text{A}}$-bound.

Although I will come to take a rather different approach to weak crossover in chapter 5, let us assume for now that the suggested approach is basically correct, and consider the analysis of examples like *Every pilot hit some MIG that chased him*. As pointed out in May (1977) and elsewhere, such sentences show an interaction of scope and anaphora; the pronoun *him* can be taken as a bound variable only if the phrase that contains it has narrower scope. On the current analysis this sentence will have the LF-representation in (3):

(3) $[_{S'}[_S$ some MIG that chased him$_3$ $[_S$ every pilot$_2$ $[_S$ e_2 hit $e_3]]]]$

In this structure, as minimally required, the pronoun is c-commanded by its putative binder *every pilot*, since S', the sole maximal projection dominating this phrase,also dominates the pronoun. But as pointed out in Koopman and Sportiche (1982), bound variable anaphora is excluded for such a structure, regardless of the scope relations of the quantifiers, since the *every*-phrase would be illicitly $\bar{A}$-binding two categories, which, *pace* Safir, are of nonparallel types. However, as Koopman and Sportiche also point out, no such violation arises in a structure, also derivable on our current assumptions, in which the object NP has been adjoined to VP rather than to S:

(4) $[_{S'} [_S$ every pilot$_2$ $[_S$ e_2 $[_{VP}$ some MIG that chased him$_3$ $[_{VP}$ hit $e_3]]]]]$

Here *every pilot* only $\bar{A}$-binds an empty category, which in turn (A-) binds the pronoun contained in the phrase that is now adjoined to VP. This pattern of binding is legitimate, being no different from the binding found in the LF-representation of *Every pilot believes that he hit some MIG*. And note that this structure exhibits no flexibility with respect to scope relations: the *every*-phrase can only be interpreted as taking broader scope.[4]

Extending the point, notice that although the above example allows bound variable anaphora under a certain scope interpretation, this is excluded in *Some pilot who shot at it hit every MIG*, regardless of scope relations. This is a case of weak crossover, and it arises because in order for the pronoun to be within the scope of *every MIG* at LF, it is necessary to move this phrase to S; if it were adjoined to VP, its scope would be required to be shorter than that of the phrase containing the pronoun. But then we find the sort of nonparallel $\bar{A}$-binding that we are taking to be proscribed; hence the exclusion of bound variable anaphora in this case.

These arguments, then, in conjunction with those tendered in the discussion of the scope interactions of *wh*- and quantified phrases, indicate the validity of assuming that QR can effect an adjunction to VP. In such positions the scope of adjoined phrases is narrower relative to the scope of phrases in COMP or of phrases adjoined to S. But there is another issue, not yet broached, regarding the absolute scope domain of such phrases. On the one hand it might be thought, naturally enough, that their scope domain is VP, since phrases in the VP-adjoined position are dominated by an occurrence of this node. But it is hard to see just what semantic sense is to be made of a quantifier having "predicate" level scope; in fact, where VP-level quantification has been employed, it has been assumed to have absolute scope no different from that of S-level quantifiers. For instance, Williams (1977) makes this claim in his discussion of VP-deletion, and Montague (1974) assumes that in the translation of VP(IV)-level quantification, the quantifier is a function whose argument contains a free variable position for the (to-be-constructed) subject, bound from outside the scope of the quantifier by an abstraction operator. This essentially equates the scope of S- and VP-quantifiers as clausal, although a VP-quantifier will have scope narrower than the subject (see Montague (1974), rules S/T16 in PTQ). In the framework adopted here, given that scope is a basically syntactic notion, the issue of the scope of VP-adjoined quantifiers reduces to the question of the c-command domain of the VP-adjoined phrase. Since this is a Chomsky-adjunction to a maximal projection (with S-adjunction a phrase is attached to an intermediary level in the projection from INFL to S'), it is important whether the nodes arising as a structural effect of LF-movement themselves constitute independent instances of maximal projections, for the definition of c-command assumed above crucially mentions "dominating maximal projection." Adopting this interpretation, however, would lead to a number of untoward consequences. Semantically, it would fix VP as the scope of VP-adjoined quantifiers and syntactically, it would violate at least the spirit of $\bar{\text{X}}$-theory, contravening the notion that in a given structure there is a one-to-one correspondence between heads and maximal projections. Let us reject this interpretation and assume instead that such nodes do not constitute distinct categorial projections, now understanding the occurrence of a *projection* (at a given bar level) to be made up of a set of occurrences of nodes that are featurally nondistinct (that is, identical with respect to syntactic features, bar level, index, etc.). It is these nodes, taken collectively, that constitute the membership of a projection. In effect, this characterization claims that the structural effect of (Chomsky)-adjunction is to create multimembered projections. This retains the central idea that there is a one-to-one relation between heads and maximal projections, although the latter may be complex, in the sense of containing a number of constituent nodes. Of course, this extends to projections of bar levels other than maximal. Thus, either lexical or medial level categories could be multimembered, as in adjunction to S in LF, or extraposition from NP constructions in S-Structure (see chapter 4).

On this interpretation of the relation between nodes and projections, derivations will be inherently "structure-preserving," in the sense that the categorial structure imposed by $\bar{\text{X}}$-theory on D-Structure representations will remain unchanged in the course of derivation via "Move α," be it onto S-Structure or LF, although the hierarchical and/or linear arrangement of constituents may be altered. What are held constant during a derivation, then, are not so much those properties ultimately contributing to the determination of weak generative capacity, but rather those contributing to a stronger notion of generative capacity pertaining to categorial structure. Eliminated, on this view, is an asymmetry often held to exist between substitutions, taken to be structure-preserving, and adjunctions, taken not to be; in fact, all movements will be structure-preserving in this sense.

It follows from this notion of projection that to be *dominated* by an occurrence of a projection, maximal or otherwise, is to be dominated by *all* the member nodes of that projection. Hence, a phrase that is Chomsky-adjoined to a given projection is *not*, in fact, dominated by that projection, but only by part of it. To see this, consider (5):

(5)

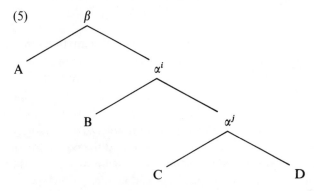

In (5) B has been adjoined to α; hence, the α-projection now consists of the two occurrences of the node α, α^i and α^j. The α-projection dominates only C and D, but not B. This is because B is dominated by only one *member* of the α-projection (i.e., α^i) and not by the entire α-projection. Rather, the minimal projection dominating B is the uniquely membered β-projection. Now, assuming that α and β are maximal projections, the c-command domain (and hence the scope, under appropriate circumstances) of B is the β-projection; it therefore includes A, C, and D, which are also dominated by this projection. The c-command domain of C is the α-projection, since it is dominated by both α^i and α^j. The latter domain includes D, but not B, which is dominated not by the α-projection but by only one of its member nodes, namely α^i.

Extending these notions to conjoined nodes, we can take a conjoining node as the intersection point of the conjoined projections. Thus, in (6) the node $\alpha^{i,j}$ is a member of both the α^i and α^j projections:

(6)

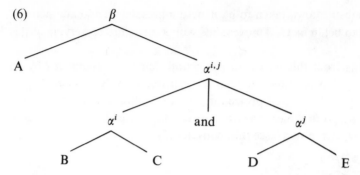

In this structure nothing dominated by α^i will c-command anything in α^j (and vice versa). C, for instance, will be dominated by the α^i-projection, which is made up of α^i and the conjoining $\alpha^{i,j}$ nodes, and nothing within the α^j-projection will also be dominated by this projection. This interpretation of the structure of conjunctions has consequences for anaphora across VP-conjuncts, predicting the ungrammaticality of *Rosa saw Oscar and kissed himself* and *Rosa saw the men and kissed each other*, and the possibility of coreference in *Mary saw Oscar and kissed him*. This is simply because the object NP in each example, which occupies the position of C in (6), does not c-command the anaphor or pronoun in the other conjunct.

Given this articulation of "projection" and its interaction with c-command, consider again a structure such as the one given schematically in (7), that is, the structure in which there is VP-adjunction. The VP-projection is as indicated:

(7)

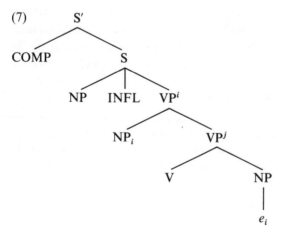

Returning now to our original question—What is the scope of NP_i, adjoined to VP?—we see that it is its c-command domain, which is S'. This maximal projection is the minimal one dominating NP_i, which is dominated not by the VP-projection, but only by its higher member node. Thus, the "absolute" scope of NP_i extends outside the VP to the clausal level as does the scope of S-adjoined quantifiers and *wh*-pharses in COMP, although, as we have seen, VP-adjoined phrases will have relative scope shorter than their counterparts in COMP or adjoined to S. This is because a maximal projection boundary, that of VP, remains between the VP- and S-adjoined positions, blocking government. The fact that VP-adjoined phrases have clausal (S') scope does not mean that they will necessarily function syntactically or semantically like S-adjoined quantified phrases. The only claim is that insofar as they do differ, the difference will not turn on whether the subject position is or is not included within the quantified phrase's scope; since both VP-adjoined and S-adjoined quantified phrases have S' as their c-command domain, they both include this position within their scopes.

Although no government relations hold between VP-adjuncts and phrases either in COMP or adjoined to S, they may still satisfy the weaker structural relation of mutual c-command. Thus, we find well-formed crossing coreference sentences like *Which pilot who shot at it hit every MIG that chased him*; recall that all that is required here is that each pronoun be properly within the scope of the quantified phrase binding it. But whereas the pronouns may be simultaneously bound, the quantifiers can only be interpreted in a fixed order; this is as expected, since at LF they fail to satisfy the Scope Principle.

Since a VP-adjoined quantifier is not technically extracted from the VP-projection, we can account for the scope properties of sentences such as *Some professor admires every student and despises the Dean* while maintaining that the Coordinate Structure Constraint holds of LF-representations. This is simply because the quantifier phrase in the initial VP-adjunct can be adjoined to VP, and need not be extracted from it in order to be adjoined to S. Notice that this sentence seems to strongly favor a specific, broad scope construal for the subject phrase (as opposed to its counterpart without the second conjunct), which is expected, since VP-adjoined quantifiers will have scope narrower than those adjoined to S.

The observation that emerges from these considerations is that even though LF-movements are free, in the sense of being instances of "Move α," the class of representations derived is in fact just those in which the extracted phrase has clausal scope. Indeed, we might take this observation to be principled by maintaining that scope domains must range over complete argument structures, and not their proper subparts. One way to capture this is to adopt the following proposition:

(8) If an operator O c-commands a predicate P, then it must
     c-command all the thematic argument positions of P.

Imposing such a condition will severely limit the class of "landing sites" for
LF-movement to, intuitively, those positions in which an operator's scope
includes all, and only, the internal and external arguments of any predicates
that operator has scope over. This will be satisfied in all the cases considered thus far of operators in $\bar{\text{A}}$-positions, regardless of whether they occur
in COMP or adjoined to S or VP, a trivial result with respect to those
predicates that are embedded below an operator occurring in one of these
positions. Moreover, because S' is a maximal projection, the c-command
domain of an operator occurring in an embedded $\bar{\text{A}}$-position is normally
prevented from extending into a higher clause, so it cannot include any
predicates occurring above it within its scope.

Notice that given the characterization of c-command there is a circumstance where the situation just described would fail to hold: namely, if a
phrase were adjoined to an embedded S' itself. Then its c-command domain
would extend beyond the S' into the higher clause, since the adjoined phrase
would fail to be dominated by the S'-projection, but would only be dominated by a member of that projection. Instead, the c-command domain of
such a phrase would be determined by the next highest maximal projection,
VP, assuming for discussion the case of object complementation. But such
a representation would then have a predicate within its scope (namely, the
head verb of the VP), but not all the arguments of the predicate; in
particular, its c-command domain would exclude the subject argument.
Thus, phrases adjoined to an embedded S' will have a status quite different
from that of phrases adjoined to S or VP or moved to COMP. Such a
structural contrast will not be found, however, with adjunction to a matrix
S'; the c-command domain of S'-adjuncts will be no different from that
arising from the other instances of LF-movement. This is because with
adjunction to the matrix S' there is *no* maximal projection dominating the
adjoined phrases, and since there are also no maximal projections dominating the root S'-projection, it follows that every maximal projection dominating the adjoined phrase also dominates S'—hence the c-command
domain of matrix S'-adjuncts is demarcated as clausal, just in the case of S
and VP adjuncts and phrases in COMP.

Now, what is to be made of this distinction? Of course, under the
interpretation of LF-movement as "Move α," extraction to the S'-adjunct

position is simply one among the available derivational options. But this does not preclude the possibility that this position is singled out by the rules that assign interpretations to the LF-representations so derived. Suppose that this is indeed what happens, and specifically that phrases in this position are interpreted as focus, so that for instance those phrases that have focal stress in S-Structure will only be assigned an appropriate interpretation in the S'-adjunct position at LF. That the S'-adjunct position is the locus of focus interpretation has been argued for extensively in Culicover and Rochement (1983). Taking this to be so, we can directly account for a certain peculiar and interesting property of focus constructions. The phenomenon I have in mind can be most clearly seen by considering embedded echo questions. That such constructions involve LF-movement can be concluded from the absence of a bound variable construal in either (9a) or (9b), given, as I have been assuming, that weak crossover is a diagnostic.

(9)a. Who did his mother see?
   b. His mother saw whó?

Apparently, the LF-movement involved in such focused constructions must be to a maximally broad scope position. Thus, (10a) and (10b) can only be construed as direct questions, with answers such as (11):

(10)a. Ehrlichman thought that Nixon did whát?
    b. Ehrlichman wondered whether Nixon did whát?

(11) Erase the White House tapes!

Or consider (12), which allows (13a), but not (13b), as an answer:

(12) Who remembered where Nixon did whát?

(13)a. Dean remembered where he erased the White House tapes.
    b. Dean did.

(13b), however, is an answer to the question identical to (12), except that the final wh-phrase is not focused.

    How then to account for this property of focus constructions? Recall our assumption that what distinguishes focused NPs from other $\bar{\text{A}}$-adjoined phrases at LF is that they are adjoined to S'. This will allow for the derivation of two LF-representations from the S-Structure representation of (10a), one by adjunction to the matrix, the other by adjunction to the complement:

(14)a. [$_{S'}$ what$_2$ [$_{S'}$ Ehrlichman thought [$_{S'}$ that Nixon did e_2]]]

   b. [$_{S'}$ Ehrlichman thought [$_{S'}$ what$_2$ [$_{S'}$ that Nixon did e_2]]]

The scope of *what* in (14a) is clearly consistent with the strictures on inclusion of argument structure; it includes within its scope all selected argument positions of the matrix and complement predicates. In (14b), on the other hand, this is not so. Since *what* in this structure is not dominated by the S'-projection, its c-command domain is delimited by the matrix VP. But this scope domain does not contain one of the matrix predicate's arguments, namely the subject. In this way we can account for the deviance of (14b), and hence the requirement for broad scope in focus constructions.

In all the cases discussed so far the complement clause is an S', a maximal projection. Note, though, that if a complement clausal node were not a maximal projection—for instance, if it were S rather than S'—we would expect effects similar to those we have been observing with adjunction to S'. This is because the c-command domain of phrases adjoined to this node will be demarcated by the next highest maximal projection, which will again be VP. Such categorial reduction of a clause boundary to S is what is hypothesized to be involved in "S'-deletion" structures in exceptional Case-marking constructions such as *Philby believes no agent to be competent to discover moles* (Chomsky (1981)). As observed in chapter 2, broad scope is favored in such sentences; indeed, some have claimed that this is the only interpretation available for this construction, as opposed to its tensed counterpart (Postal (1974, 222), although the facts are perhaps less than clear here). Parallel properties are found in perception verb constructions with small clause complements such as *Philby observed somebody spying*; see Chomsky (1981), Stowell (1983), and Higginbotham (1983a) for arguments, based on Case and anaphoric opacity, that such constructions involve government of the complement subject by the higher predicate across a nonmaximal projection. Barwise (1981) notes that the quantified phrase in such sentences is construed as having broad scope, entailing that there is a particular person whom Philby observed spying. This observation now follows, since to adjoin the quantified phrase to the embedded S would entail its having scope over the higher predicate *observe*, but not over the subject of this predicate. Consequently, it must be adjoined within the higher clause, a position from which it c-commands both the higher predicate and its subject.[5]

We have seen that under the characterization of the relation of nodes and projections it follows that VP-adjoined quantified phrases have clausal scope, a fact that need not be stipulated, since it is now simply a consequence of the syntax of LF-representations. Assuming further that such clausal scope is in fact required also explained the absence of narrow scope construals in focus constructions, an account that turned once again on the view that projections may be complex, with c-command requiring domination by every member node of a maximal projection. In altering the assessment of c-command, this articulation of the notions of nodes and projections will also alter government relations, given that the latter notion minimally involves symmetrical c-command. For instance, any number of phrases adjoined to a single projection will govern one another, regardless of whether they are adjoined to a maximal projection or not, since none of the phrases will be dominated by that projection itself. Indeed, we availed ourselves of this fact in formulating the Scope Principle. Further government properties of adjoined phrases can be seen by considering the relations that hold among the nodes and projections depicted in (5), repeated here:

(5)

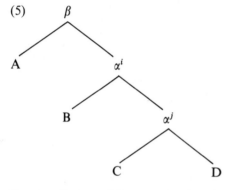

Suppose that α and β are maximal projections, the former consisting of two nodes, the latter of just one. In this structure the adjoined phrase B will not be governed by C, because C fails to c-command B, although B will be governed by the α-projection (as will A). This is because β is the only maximal projection dominating B and the α-projection, consisting of the nodes α^i, α^j, and B (recall that the α-projection does not dominate B). Moreover, there is no maximal projection boundary between α and B, since B is in fact contained *within* the boundaries of the α-projection. Thus, the structural government relations between α and B are no different than those between α and A; in this case as well only β dominates each, and no maximal projection boundaries intervene to interfere with government.

These characterizations of government relations will also have a number of consequences for VP-adjuncts, especially as they occur in S-Structure representations. For instance, it is generally assumed that subject θ-roles are assigned by VP to NPs they govern, which is unproblematic for [NP,S] subjects (Chomsky (1981)). Certain languages, however, allow "free inversion" of the subject to the VP-adjoined position. For example, in Italian *Gianni arriva* 'Gianni arrives' cooccurs with *Arriva Gianni*, the latter having the structure in (15) (leaving open for the time being the exact identity of the subject empty category):

(15) [$_S$ e [$_{VP}$[$_{VP}$ arriva] Gianni]]

In this structure the VP governs the VP-adjoined NP; as noted, this is because S' is the only maximal projection dominating both the VP-projection and the NP, and no maximal projection boundaries intervene between them. This circumstance corresponds to the one described abstractly above regarding the relation of the α-projection and B in (5). Thus, a VP-adjoined phrase can just as well be taken as "subject" for θ-role assignment as its nonpostposed counterpart. English also has a construction—the presentational *there*-sentence—in which the subject occurs post verbally, adjoined to VP. As an example of this type of structure consider (16):

(16)

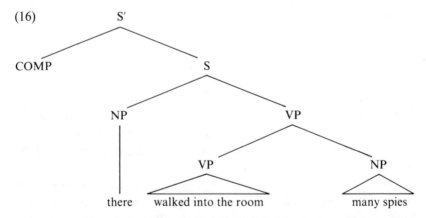

Again, note that the VP-adjoined NP is just as much governed in this structure by the VP-projection as is the [NP,S] position of *there*. This is because the only maximal projection dominating the postposed NP is S', which is also the sole maximal projection dominating VP. Here too no maximal projection boundary intervenes between VP and the postverbal NP, since the latter phrase is contained within the VP. Therefore, in this structure also the postposed position can be taken as just as much a "subject" position for θ-role assignment from VP as the preverbal position.

Though the VP-adjoined position is a legitimate position for θ-role assignment in structures like (15) and (16), this will not be the case for the VP-adjoined position occupied by a quantified phrase that has been moved from some embedded position and attached to VP. Such phrases will not be assigned a subject θ-role; if they were, the θ-Criterion would be violated, since they also bind empty categories that themselves occur in thematic positions.

The postposed subject position, then, will in general have the same structural properties as the normal subject; in particular, it will not be c-commanded by V, since V is dominated by a maximal projection, VP, which does not dominate the NP (although the NP does c-command V). This allows us to directly account for some facts about Italian brought to light by Belletti and Rizzi (1982) and Burzio (1981). Italian has a clitic, *ne* 'of-them', which can be attached to V, as in sentences like (17):

(17) Gianni ne   transcorrerà tre   a Milano.
     Gianni of them will spend   three in Milan
     'Gianni will spend three of them in Milan.'

(17), however, contrasts with (18), in which *ne* has been extracted from a subject, rather than an object, NP:

(18) *Tre ne   passano rapidamente.
      three of-them pass   rapidly

Belletti and Rizzi attribute this distinction to the fact that *ne* c-commands its trace only when extracted from an object; thus, the ungrammaticality of (18) results from a failure of proper binding.

As for postverbal subjects, Italian has two types, one in which the postverbal NP is adjoined to VP, the other in which it is in a position structurally nondistinct from that of a transitive object. Among the arguments for this distinction brought out by Belletti and Rizzi is that the two types of structures can be distinguished in part by the auxiliaries with which they cooccur, the former being found with *avere*, the latter with *essere*. With respect to *ne*-cliticization, the two types of postverbal subjects pattern like preverbal subjects and objects, respectively:

(19) *Ne   hanno parlato tre.
      of-them have   spoken three

(20)   Ne   sono arrivati tre.
       of-them have arrived three

These sentences have the structures indicated in (21) and (22), respectively:

(21) $[e \, [_{VP}[_{VP} \, ne_i + V \ldots] \, [_{NP} \, Q \, e_i]]]$

(22) $[e \, [_{VP} \, ne_i + V \ldots [_{NP} \, Q \, e_i]]]$

Since *ne* is attached to V in (19), it does not c-command its trace, contained in the VP-adjoined NP. This is because VP dominates the former, but not the latter. Here, then, as with the [NP, S] subject, there is a failure of proper binding. In (20), on the other hand, *ne* does c-command its trace, which is in a position structurally nondistinct from that of the object in (17). Thus, on our view the structural relations between *ne* and its trace are quite the same in (19) and (20) as in (17) and (18).

Since V does not c-command the VP-adjoined position, by extension it does not *govern* this position, since government minimally requires mutual c-command. Consequently, we would not expect any movement to be possible from the position of NP in (16), for instance, since, this position not being governed, it is not properly governed. This is corroborated by the impossibility of *wh*-movement in presentational *there*-sentences; for instance, note the contrast between (23a) and (23b):

(23)a. *I didn't realize how many spies there had walked into the room from Russia.
     b.   I didn't realize that there had walked into the room so many spies from Russia.[6]

In contrast, *wh*-movement is possible with minimally contrasting existentials:

(24) I didn't realize how many spies there were from Russia.

Here, assuming that Stowell (1978, 1983) is correct, the trace of the *wh*-phrase, which is the subject of a small clause complement, is governed by the copula, which constitutes proper government. Notice that this circumstance will also allow for LF-movement from this position when there has not been *wh*-movement. However, QR to S will be blocked for presentationals, just as for *wh*-movement, by the ECP. In this case we can simply assume that QR is to VP, giving (25) as the LF-representation derived from (16):

(25)

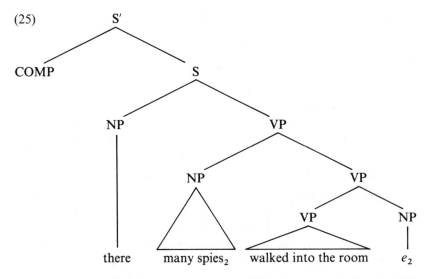

In this structure the phrase *many spies* will bind, as a variable, the VP-adjoined empty category, which is a θ-position (and presumably an A-position, being for all intents and purposes the subject of the sentence). Moreover, (25) will be consistent with the ECP, falling under the coindexing clause of this condition. Recall that government will hold between phrases adjoined to members of a single projection; since both *many spies* and its trace are adjoined to VP, this example illustrates the circumstance in which proper government holds between coindexed phrases, one of which occurs in an $\bar{\text{A}}$-position, the other in an A-position. Thus, here as well we are taking postposed subjects to be structurally parallel to [NP, S], in this case with regard to proper government when the latter type of subject is bound from the S-adjoined position, after QR, or from COMP, after *wh*-movement.

The Scope of NP-Adjunction

From this articulation of the notion of projection it follows that although the syntactic properties of LF may be seen to vary—mainly as a function of the derivational freedom permitted by taking LF-movement as more broadly instantiating the general properties of "Move α"—the semantically relevant properties it represents remain constant, in that both VP- and S-adjuncts demarcate their scope at the clausal level. By extension, we might expect that LF-movement, in fact, can be to any position for which this is so. In this light, consider examples like (26), which (as discussed extensively in May (1977)) admit of a construal in which the quantified phrase embedded in S-Structure has broader scope:

(26) Somebody from every city despises it.

That such sentences exhibit "inverse linking" of the quantified phrases can be seen most graphically by observing that in (26) the pronoun is properly interpreted as a variable bound by *every city*. Corroboration of the bound variable status of the pronoun arises from an observation by Reinhart (1983), who points out that there is a correspondence between positions of bound variables and the possibility of sloppy identity in deletion contexts; a similar observation is made by Lasnik (1976). Thus, contrast (27) with (28):

(27) Los Angeles is adored by its residents, and so is New York.

(28) The people who were born in Los Angeles adore its beaches, but the people who were born in New York do not.

Although the elliptical conjunct in (27) can be understood with a sloppy construal—that is, that New York is adored by New York's residents—the one in (28) cannot be construed in this way. The latter has only the nonsloppy construal, whereby New York natives are nonadorers of Los Angeles's beaches. Given Reinhart's claim, this means that the pronoun *it* can be bound as a bound variable pronoun from the position of *Los Angeles* in (27), but not in (28). Applying Reinhart's diagnostic, consider the possibility of sloppy identity in (29), that is, taking the elliptical conjunct to mean that every resident of Tokyo rides Tokyo's subways:[7]

(29) Nobody from New York rides its subways, but everybody from Tokyo does.

Given the reliability of Reinhart's diagnostic, the existence of this interpretation shows that the pronoun in (26) is a bound variable, and hence that it must be c-commanded, at LF, by the quantified phrase that binds it.

It is important not to confuse the sort of anaphora in (26) with "donkey-sentence" pronouns, that is, the sort of anaphoric relation found in sentences like *Every owner of a donkey beats it*. Although I will argue below that such sentences do evidence a form of bound anaphora, they nonetheless have somewhat different properties than the bound variable pronouns currently under discussion. For instance, insofar as a donkey-pronoun is possible with an *every*-phrase as antecedent, the pronoun must be plural. Thus, *The guy who owns every donkey beats them* contrasts with the impossibility of any sort of anaphoric relation in *The guy who owns every donkey beats it*. But note that in (26) anaphora is possible between an *every*-

phrase and a singular pronoun; this is a hallmark of bound variable anaphora as opposed to donkey-pronoun anaphora. Since we are dealing with two distinct paradigms of anaphora, I will at this point set donkey-pronouns aside for later consideration.

In the aforementioned analysis of May (1977), I proposed that the inversely linked construal of (26) be represented at LF by a structure in which the embedded quantified phrase, *every city*, is extracted from NP and adjoined to S. This seemed to be required in order to bring the pronoun within the scope of the *every*-phrase. But this raises a problem, not adequately answered in May (1977): Why can QR extract a phrase from NP in mapping onto LF, but *wh*-movement cannot, in mapping onto S-Structure? In (30a), the structure of *Which city does somebody from despise it*, there is just as much binding into NP, an island, as in (30b), the LF-representation of (26):[8]

(30)a. $[_{S'}$ which city$_2$ $[_S[_{NP}$ somebody from $e_2]$ despises it]]
    b. $[_S$ every city$_2$ $[_S[_{NP}$ somebody from $e_2]_3$ $[_S$ e_3 despises it]]]

A dilemma of sorts arises. On the one hand, (30b) allows for the proper classification of *it* as a bound variable pronoun, since it is within the scope of *every city*, but on the other hand, this phrase seems to bind into an island just as illicitly as the *wh*-phrase in (30a). The root of this problem lies in the assumption that QR must adjoin the S-Structure embedded quantifier phrase to S in order to represent the appropriate scope properties. But we are no longer assuming that LF-movement is so restricted; in fact, we are exploring the hypothesis that "Move α" can be more freely instantiated at LF. This allows us to consider an alternative analysis, namely that the LF-representation (26) involves adjunction not to S, but to NP, so that its structure at LF will be (31), not (30b):

(31)

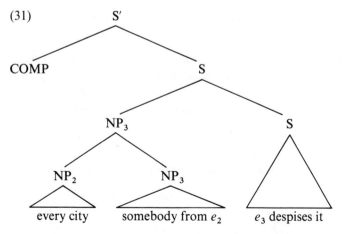

(31) arises from adjoining the embedded NP to the NP that contains it, the latter node itself being adjoined to S. Thus, there has been no extraction from NP. Both NP_2 and NP_3 will have clausal scope; note that NP_2 is *not* dominated by the NP_3 *projection*, but, as with VP-adjuncts, by only one of its constituent nodes. S′ therefore demarcates the c-command domain of NP_2, as it also does for NP_3. In particular, this domain includes the pronoun *it*, which therefore resides within the scope of *every city*. Thus, under the assumption that (31) is the proper LF-representation, the dilemma dissolves. The pronoun is correctly represented as a bound variable, without extracting from NP; NP_2 remains within the confines of NP_3 and is not extracted from this island, although its scope extends beyond. The analysis extends directly to more complex examples of inverse linking, such as *A friend of somebody from every city despises it*. Here the *some*-phrase will be adjoined to the *a*-phrase, itself adjoined to S, and the *every*-phrase will in turn be adjoined to the *some*-phrase. From this position it will c-command the pronoun *it*, which can then be interpreted as a bound variable.[9]

That inverse linking involves adjunction to NP affords an account of (32):

(32) What does somebody from every city despise?

The observation here is that even if the *every*-phrase is construed with scope wider than the *some*-phrase, it must have scope narrower than the *wh*-phrase. This is in contrast to *What does everybody despise*, in which these two phrases may arrange themselves in either scope order. (32) will be univocally interpreted just in case there fails to be government between the *every*-phrase and the *wh*-phrase; but this is just what we find, on the assumption that inverse linking involves adjunction to NP:

(33) $[_{S'}$ what$_2$ $[_S[_{NP}$ every city$_3$ $[_{NP}$ somebody from $e_3]_4][_S$ e_4 despises $e_2]]]$

Here a maximal projection boundary, that of NP_4, intervenes, and hence blocks government, between *what* and *every city*. Scope, then, is a function of constituency, and therefore the *wh*-phrase will have broader scope.

That the c-command domain of NP-adjoined quantified phrases extends to S′ is further illustrated by the possibility of crossed binding in sentences like (34):

(34) Some pilot who shot at it hit the navigator of every MIG that chased him.

The necessary condition for occurrence of crossed binding is mutual c-command, as discussed above. This will be satisfied in the LF-representation of (34) because S' will delimit the c-command domain of both *some pilot who shot at it*, adjoined to S, and *every MIG that chased him*, adjoined to NP, the latter phrase itself adjoined to S. Mutual c-command will equally well be found when this NP must be adjoined to VP, as in (35), with the LF-representation (36):

(35) Which pilot who shot at it hit the navigator of every MIG that chased him?

(36) $[_{S'}$[which pilot who shot at it]$_2$ $[_S$ e_2 hit $[_{VP}[_{NP}$ [every MIG that chased him]$_4$ $[_{NP}$ the navigator of $e_4]]_3$ $[_{VP}$ hit $e_3]]]]$

In this structure *every MIG that chased him* is dominated by both an NP and a VP node, but neither makes up the entirety of its projection. Therefore, its c-command domain is again S'.

The analysis of inverse linking carries over directly to multiple interrogation sentences such as *Which person from which city despises it*, whose LF-derivation will differ from that of (31) only in that NP-adjunction will be to a phrase already in COMP, as in (37),

(37) $[_{S'}[_{NP}$ which city$_2$ $[_{NP}$ which person from $e_2]_3]_3$ $[_S$ e_3 despises it]]$

and extends to the LF-representation of mixed quantifier-*wh* sentences such as *How many representatives from each city voted for the amendment*. This question displays the "collection of questions" construal characteristic of the *wh*-phrase having narrower scope, which is to be represented by adjoining *each city*, within COMP, to NP.

Summarizing to this point, if we assume that LF-movement exhibits more generally the properties of "Move α," the option exists, exploited in representing inverse linking NPs, of adjunction to, rather than extraction from, NP. Given the characterization of nodes and projections, and their relation to c-command, this allows for the proper determination of scope in these constructions, without the necessity of extraction from a syntactic island. The option of NP adjunction, however, is not available for *wh*-movement, which is required to be to COMP at S-Structure. Both structures in (30) may now be taken to be ill-formed, each exhibiting an illicit extraction from a syntactic island.

I have primarily concerned myself with inverse linking in complex noun phrase constructions in order to bring out two central points. One pertains to the syntax of Logical Form: the role of NP-adjunction in the characterization of this interpretation serves to confirm the generality of application of LF-movement. The second is that inverse linking serves as an existence argument for the level of LF itself, based on the observation that bound variable anaphora is found in sentences such as *Somebody from every city despises it*. Only in its representation at this level is the pronoun within the c-command domain of a binding quantified phrase, a necessary condition for bound variable anaphora. Concomitantly, such cases indicate the inadequacy of the view that quantifier scope and the possibility of bound variable anaphora are calculated in terms of S-Structure c-command relations. Although to a large extent LF and S-Structure constituency mirror one another, since LF is the image of S-Structure, closed under transformational mappings, the scope and binding properties of the above type of example show that it would be a mistake to identify them. This is because it is only in the syntax of LF that *every city* c-commands *it*; at S-Structure it simply does not.[10]

My focusing on inverse linking to establish these points should not obscure the fact that adjunction to nodes other than NP in complex noun phrases will give rise to well-formed interpretations, or that the sort of bound anaphora found with inverse linking of quantifiers is the only sort of pronominal binding found in this construction. With respect to the former, Fiengo and Higginbotham (1980) have proposed that the proper representation of what was dubbed the "relative" interpretation in May (1977), in which the scope of the S-Structure embedded quantified phrase is contained in NP, and which is thus narrower than the head phrase, involves adjunction to nodes *within* NP. This interpretation is found most naturally in examples like *Every house near a river faces danger from flooding* or *The head of every public authority in New York was Robert Moses*, and many examples are ambiguous between this construal and inverse linking. A natural assumption is that the LF-representation of the relative construal involves attachment to PP, a possible adjunction site given that LF-movement can freely adjoin, and comparable to adjunction to the internal S or VP (depending upon whether *wh*-movement has been from subject or object) in relative clauses.[11] NP-internal scope is also found in nominalizations like *Everyone living in some Italian city admires art*. But here adjunction must be to VP, not PP. If it were to the latter node, the adjoined phrase would c-command the predicate, but not its subject, *everyone*. With adjunction to either PP or VP, though, the higher NP will delimit the c-command domain of the adjoined phrase—as with all adjunctions to maximal projections, the phrase adjoined to does not dominate the adjunct—and scope therefore will not extend outside of the complex noun phrase. Note also that the two quantified phrases in the above examples will not be subject to the Scope Principle, since the projection boundaries of PP and VP block the required government; hence, the internally adjoined phrase must have narrower scope.

Turning now to bound anaphora, we may consider an additional form of pronominal binding in complex noun phrases, namely "donkey-sentences," like *Everyone who owns a donkey beats it*, brought to light in the modern literature by Geach (1962) and subsequently widely discussed.[12] That the interpretation of donkey-sentences is distinct from that of inverse linking sentences can be garnered from *Every owner of a donkey beats it*, which is ambiguous between these interpretations. On the inverse linking construal a single, communally owned donkey is beaten, whereas on the donkey-sentence construal each donkey owner beats (all) his individually owned donkeys. The problem here is to be able to distinguish these two types of interpretation, while still representing at LF that they each contain bound pronouns, which must be $\bar{\text{A}}$-bound at this level.

A solution to this puzzle can be developed based on ideas of Heim (1982). Adapting a notion from Lewis (1975), she suggests that natural language quantifiers are "unselective." That is, when a quantifier is interpreted, it can bind any variable free within its scope that has not otherwise been assigned a value. In the case of donkey-sentences like *Everyone who owns a donkey beats it*, Heim suggests that the indefinite determiner is interpreted not as a quantifier, but as a variable. Since this variable is not otherwise bound and resides within the scope of *every*, it may be selected, at all of its occurrences, by this quantifier, resulting in a complex "pair" quantifier. This gives the interpretation represented in (38):

(38) $\forall x,y$ (y is a donkey & x owns y) (x beats y)

The intended truth-conditions require that for every pair of donkey owner and donkey, the former beats the latter. The virtue of this treatment is that now if a donkey owner treats even one of his donkeys kindly, the donkey-sentence will be false. Note that in this logical form the variable corresponding to the pronoun will be bound by the derived pair quantifier.

The notion of unselective quantifiers can be incorporated within the context of the structure and interpretation of LF as follows. Let us say that in the interpretation of an LF-representation associated with the Σ-sequence $\{Q_1, \ldots, Q_n\}$, a quantifier Q_i ($1 \leq i \leq n$), under a particular scope ordering, *selects* that variable index which it is assigned under LF-movement and may (optionally) select the variable indices assigned to any other members of the sequence so long as (i) the quantifiers bearing those

Chapter 3   74

indices have narrower scope than Q_i and (ii) the additionally selected variables are free within the scope of Q_i. If the index of a quantifier Q_j is selected by another quantifier Q_i, then Q_j is interpreted as an open sentence containing an occurrence of x_j free, as suggested by Heim (although I differ from her in holding that this variable can only arise as an occurrence of an antecedently selected variable). The derived n-place quantifier will be interpreted by an n-place quantification. To illustrate, a pair universal quantifier—that is, one that selects a single additional variable aside from the one selected in virtue of its QR indexing—will be interpreted by

$$\textbf{Every}_{i,j}\,(X,\,Y) = 1 \text{ iff } X = X \cap Y$$
$$= 0 \text{ otherwise,}$$

which corresponds to the singulary quantification

$$\textbf{Every}_i\,(X,\,Y) = 1 \text{ iff } X = X \cap Y$$
$$= 0 \text{ otherwise,}$$

differing only in that the values of X, Y are subsets of ordered pairs of the domain D, the relationship between these sets required for truth remaining unchanged.[13]

With this background, consider the treatment of donkey-sentences, restricting our attention to cases in which the containing NP is a standard quantifier. What I shall propose (here departing from Heim's syntactic assumptions) it that in the sort of NP-adjoined structure we have been considering in this chapter the quantifiers may vary in scope, in accordance with the Scope Principle, and that the inversely linked and donkey interpretations are just the interpretations corresponding to the allowable scope orderings. The former will arise if the NP-adjoined quantified phrase is taken with broader scope, the latter if it is taken with narrower scope. To see this, consider the Scope Principle and its consequences for interpretation when applied to (39), the LF-representation of *Every owner of a donkey beats it*:

(39) $[_{S'}[_S[_{NP}$ a donkey$_2$ $[_{NP}$ every owner of $e_2]]_3$ $[_S\ e_3$ beats it$_2]]]$

Since both NP$_2$, *a donkey*, and NP$_3$, *every owner of e_2*, have S' as their only dominating maximal projection (NP$_2$ not being dominated by the NP$_3$-projection, but only one of its member nodes), and since there is no maximal projection boundary between NP$_2$ and NP$_3$ (the boundaries of the higher NP-projection being demarcated by its leftmost and rightmost brackets), government obtains, and NP$_2$ and NP$_3$ form a Σ-sequence. Consequently, (39) may be interpreted with the quantifiers in either scope order. Suppose that NP_2, *a donkey* (or *every city* in (31) for that matter), is taken with broader scope. Then we simply have the inversely linked interpretation. On the other hand, what if the other quantified phrase, *every owner of* e_2, is taken with broader scope? As it stands, this scope ordering will not lead to a determinate interpretation, since the broad scope quantifier will contain a variable, "e_2," which does not otherwise receive an assignment, since it is, on this ordering, outside the scope of *a donkey*. But if quantifiers are unselective this can be overcome, since *every* can now select this variable, of which the pronoun *it* is an occurrence, in addition to the variable with which it is coindexed by virtue of QR.[14] The resulting interpretively derived pair quantifier will contain within its (semantic) scope those elements that are $\bar{A}$-bound at LF by the *every*-phrase and by the *a*-phrase. It only remains to take the latter indefinite phrase as an open sentence to arrive at the interpretation, given in logical notation in (38), in which the value of X in the universal pair quantification given above will be

$$\{\langle x, y \rangle | \ y \text{ is a donkey } \& \ x \text{ owns } y\},$$

whereas that of Y will be

$$\{\langle x, y \rangle | \ x \text{ beats } y\},$$

and it will be true if and only if the former set is identical to its intersection with the latter. And this will be so just in case each and every donkey owner beats each and every one of the donkeys he owns.

What are the extent and limitations of the derivation and interpretation of pair quantifiers? One limitation arises from the constraints placed on the formation of multiple quantifiers by clauses (i) and (ii) above, which ensure that any additionally selected variables would not otherwise be assigned values in the course of interpretation. Thus, the quantifiers in a simple multiply quantified sentence like *Every student admires a professor* must have their normal, singulary interpretation. This is a welcome result, for a paired universal interpretation would entail that all of the professors are admired, a consequence this sentence lacks on any of its interpretations. Similarly, no additional variable selection beyond the one indicated directly in the LF-representation is possible for inverse linking, for again neither clause (i) nor clause (ii) is satisfied by either variable. Another limitation arises from the fact that pair quantifications apply only when the expressions within the scope of the pair quantifier are satisfied by sets of ordered pairs, that is, when they contain two distinct variable positions free. This leaves open the possibility that although an LF-representation may otherwise display the structural configuration necessary for a pair quantifier, a pair interpretation may still not be forthcoming if the derived quantifier does not otherwise contain the requisite variables within its scope. Illustrating this are examples like (40), due to Haïk (1984), in which a donkey interpretation is apparently excluded:

(40) Your shouting at every owner of a donkey frightened it.

To see this we need only observe that the position of the complex noun phrase in (40) is a "scope island"; an anaphoric interpretation is just as much excluded for a simple quantifier, as in *Your shouting at everyone frightened him.* But if the scope of *every owner of a donkey* is contained within the gerund, then it cannot include the pronoun *it* within its scope. In that case it cannot be interpreted as a pair quantifier, for it is only by binding this pronoun that it can come to have the second variable position within its scope; consequently, the possibility of a donkey interpretation is excluded. Of course, this is not to say that donkey interpretations are always unavailable if the NP containing the antecedent is embedded. Consider (41), which does allow this sort of anaphora:

(41) A friend of every owner of a donkey beats it.

In this case *every owner of a donkey* may be adjoined to the containing NP, a position from which it will c-command *it*. That is, a donkey interpretation is possible just in case the subject NP is understood with inversely linked quantifiers, and this in fact accords with our judgment on these examples.[15]

One way we may seek to extend the treatment of donkey-sentences is by allowing not just indefinite phrases to be interpreted as open sentences, as in Heim (1982), but any quantifier phrase, so that the account can be generalized to a broader class of cases. Thus, whereas *a donkey* in the interpretation of *Every owner of a donkey beats it* translates as "x is a donkey," *every donkey* in the interpretation of *Every owner of every donkey beats them* translates as "x is every donkey," the satisfiers of which are sets containing all of the donkeys in the domain. Thus, the above sentence will be true just in case for each pairing of a donkey owner and the totality of donkeys, the former beats the latter. Now, I will call the "semantic" number of a variable *singular* if it can be satisfied by singleton sets, *plural* if it must be satisfied by sets of greater cardinality, and *undefined* otherwise. Pronouns functioning as bound variables must agree with other occurrences in number. It now follows that the pronoun in a universal donkey-sentence must be plural, so that no donkey interpretation is found in *Everybody who owns every donkey beats it*, with a singular pronoun, or in *The owner of every car sold it*, which is uniquely interpreted as inversely linked (as opposed to *The owner of every car sold them*, which has solely the donkey interpretation). A further consequence is the absence of donkey anaphora in *Everybody who owns no donkey beat it*; since the derived predicate here will have the null set as its extension, it is undefined for semantic number, and there can be no agreement with the pronoun.

To summarize, the LF-representation of inverse linking sentences and donkey-sentences is identical: at this level both types of interpretation are represented by an NP-adjoined structure. This accounts for the occurrence of bound variable pronouns in either type of interpretation. The difference between them corresponds to the different scope orderings of the quantifiers in complex noun phrases permissible under the Scope Principle, which, in conjunction with the notion that quantifiers are unselective, leads to the distinct interpretations. In inverse linking the quantifiers select only those variables with which they are coindexed at LF, whereas in donkey-sentences there is a variable free that may be additionally selected by the broader scope quantifier. This gives rise to the pair quantifiers that account for the characteristic semantic properties of this construction.

Leaving the discussion of donkey-sentences and turning to another type of complex noun phrase construction, we find that in possessive sentences, as in PP-complements, a quantifier embedded in what is a syntactic island for *wh*-movement can bind a phrase outside its S-Structure c-command domain. Thus, observe the possibility of interpreting the pronouns in *Everyone's mother saw him/his brother* as bound variables.[16] Analytically, we can assume here as well that what is involved is adjunction to NP, as in (42):

(42) [$_S$[$_{NP}$ everyone$_2$ [$_{NP}$ e_2's mother]] saw him/his brother]

As before, the NP-adjoined quantifier will now c-command the pronouns; not being dominated by the projection to which it is adjoined, its scope domain is marked off by S'. With this construction as well the analysis can be carried over directly to phrases in COMP, so that in the LF-representation of *Whose mother saw him/his brother* the pronouns will be within the scope of the *wh*-phrase adjoined to NP in COMP.

Notice that in (42) there has simply been adjunction to NP; the phrase containing the embedded quantifier has not itself been moved to S. Nor is there reason to assume that any such further movement takes place, since (42) will have the appropriate structural properties as is. In this regard possessive NPs differ from PP complements that contain further quantified phrases and thus require further movement. However, when we turn our attention to possessive phrases in object, rather than subject, position, a somewhat different treatment is required. Thus, consider (43), in which there has simply been adjunction to NP in deriving an LF-representation for *Dulles suspected every country's agents*:

(43) Dulles [$_{VP}$ suspected [$_{NP}$ every country$_2$ [$_{NP}$ e_2's agents]]]

In this structure the c-command domain of the NP-adjoined phrase is VP, not S', since VP is the initial maximal projection dominating this phrase. Thus, its domain illicitly includes a predicate but not all of its arguments. Given that (43) is ill-formed, this means that the phrase *every country* must be moved to a position in which it can have scope at the S' level; that is, it must be attached to S. To attach it to S, however, requires pied piping the containing NP, since otherwise the derivation would involve an illicit extraction from an island. Consequently, the LF-representation must be as in (44):

(44) [$_S$[$_{NP}$ every country$_2$ [$_{NP}$ e_2's agents]]$_3$ [$_S$ Dulles suspected e_3]]

There is some evidence that this type of structure is appropriate. Bach and Partee (1980), noting the example in (45), point out that it is the entire NP that has broad scope, not simply the embedded possessive phrase:

(45) At least three professors read every candidate's thesis.

This follows on our analysis, since it is only the containing NP that will govern the other quantified phrase; the NP-adjoined phrase at LF will not, since government will be blocked by the boundary of the NP to which it is adjoined. Further evidence for this contention is found in the contrast between (46a) and (46b):

(46)a. His picture of her disturbed John's wife.
     b. Whose wife did his picture of her disturb?

It seems that although both pronouns can be construed anaphorically in (46a), neither pronoun can be so understood in (46b); that is, weak crossover affects *both* pronouns in the latter sentence. This follows on the assumption that, at LF, both *whose* and e_2's wife will illicitly bind both an empty category and a pronoun. Now consider (47):

(47) His picture of her disturbed everyone's wife.

The judgments here apparently parallel those made for (46b); that is, anaphora is excluded for both pronouns. But this is just the parallelism we would expect, given that the LF-representation of (47) will be of the sort illustrated in (44), a structure that will be the same as the one assigned to (46b) in the relevant respects, and hence will give rise to weak crossover violations.

Crossover phenomena in these constructions warrant more consideration before continuing, however. Recall that we are assuming that weak crossover violations arise whenever there is a typological asymmetry in multiple $\bar{A}$-binding; but note that not only the LF-representation of *Whose brother did his mother see at the baseball stadium* will exhibit this property, but also the representation of *Whose mother saw his brother at the baseball stadium*:

(48)a. $[_{S'}[_{NP}$ who$_2$ $[_{NP}$ e_2's mother]]$_3$ $[_S$ e_3 saw his$_2$ brother at the baseball stadium]]

    b. $[_{S'}[_{NP}$ who$_2$ $[_{NP}$ e_2's mother]]$_3$ $[_S$ his$_2$ brother saw e_3 at the baseball stadium]]

It would seem that in neither structure should it be possible to construe the pronoun as a bound variable. Positional approaches to weak crossover fare no better, making the opposite claim, since in either structure the pronoun stands to the right of its empty category "antecedent." The same holds for strong crossover when a pronoun is substituted for the possessive phrase.

One proposal suggested in the literature to treat these cases of crossover involves "reconstruction": the idea, deriving from suggestions in Chomsky (1977), that the effects of pied piping on *wh*-movement are undone at LF. On this view the relevant LF-representations are not those in (48), but rather those in (49):

(49)a. [whose$_2$ [e_2's mother saw his brother at the baseball stadium]]

    b. [whose$_2$ [his brother saw e_2's mother at the baseball stadium]]

Thus, only in (49b) will an operator directly $\bar{A}$-bind both a lexical pronoun and an empty category (or, if a positional account is preferred, only in (49b) will the pronoun stand to the left of its antecedent). However, as brought out by Higginbotham (1980), this sort of account can be shown to be unworkable. Higginbotham points out that parallel examples can be constructed with inverse linking in PP-complements, bound variable anaphora being found only in the (a) example:

(50)a. Which driver of which millionaire's car was hired by his father?

    b. Which driver of which millionaire's car did his father hire?

Reconstruction will give, roughly, the structures in (51):

(51)a. [$_{S'}$ which millionaire$_2$ [$_S$ which driver of e_2's car was hired by his
   father]]
   b. [$_{S'}$ which millionaire$_2$ [$_S$ his father hired which driver of e_2's car]]

The problem is that after reconstruction LF-movement must apply again,
if the constraint on multiple interrogation—that all of the *wh*-phrases must
occur in a [+WH] COMP at LF—is to be satisfied. But this further
movement would just reinstate the problem. Higginbotham points out that
the same paradoxical result is found with non-*wh* quantifiers, since bound
variable anaphora is excluded in *It is despised by somebody from every city*,
as opposed to *Somebody from every city despises it*.

Higginbotham (1980, 1983b) and Safir (1984) suggest that the anaphoric
asymmetry of the "reconstruction" cases be handled by a condition that
rules out structures containing binding configurations of the form

$$\ldots[_j\ldots i\ldots]\ldots j\ldots i\ldots$$

Though the particular conditions that have been suggested turn out to be of
no more than a descriptive nature, assuming such a proscription does allow
us to maintain LF-representations such as (48) and (51), eschewing any
dubious sort of structural reconstruction.[17] However, rather than explore
the exact content of the proposed conditions, I will leave this topic for the
time being, deferring further discussion to chapter 5. There we will see that
under the constraints on LF-representations to be developed, the properties of bound variable anaphora in these cases will follow directly.

Returning now to the main thread of this section: What constrains
movement from syntactic islands such as PP-complements and possessive
NPs, for both S-Structure and LF-movement? One possibility is a constraint applying to extraction and/or its traces generally, such as Subjacency. It is difficult to see how such a constraint can be properly imple-
mented, however, in that LF-movement can effect cyclic adjunctions, each
of which is consistent with Subjacency (see chapter 4). Moreover, there are
apparently LF-movements that can, in certain circumstances, extract from
NP. One case is brought up by Van Riemsdijk and Williams (1981), who
point out that a question such as *Who knows which pictures of whom Bill
bought* allows an interpretation in which *whom* is paired with *who* in asking
a multiple direct question. Representing this, on the view here, involves
extracting from an island, so as to move *whom* to a higher clause, as shown
in (52):

(52) [$_{S'}$ whom$_3$ who$_2$ [$_S$ e_2 knows [$_{S'}$ [which pictures of e_3]$_4$ [$_S$ Bill bought
   e_4]]]]

Thus, although we might hold that Subjacency requires that any extraction take place via cyclic adjunctions, it cannot be so construed as to block movement from NP at LF.[18] (We will return to this in the context of the analysis of extraposition in chapter 4, where we will also see certain other cases in which there is extraction from NP in LF.) And indeed examples of this sort indicate that even a constraint that proscribes movement to a position outside of NP regardless of cyclicity of application, such as Kayne's (1981b) extended ECP, could not be precisely correct, if LF-movements are treated as strictly on a par with movements onto S-Structure with regard to island contexts.

Let us consider, then, a rather different approach proposed by Guéron and May (1984), elaborating a suggestion of Stowell (1981): namely, that only one operator can be adjoined per projection level (the intent being to allow just one $\bar{\text{A}}$-position at any given level of an $\bar{\text{X}}$-projection). The singulary occurrence of COMP, the $\bar{\text{A}}$-position of S', is a paradigmatic example. This constraint, it might be presumed, would be a theorem of a properly formulated $\bar{\text{X}}$-theory of categories.

An immediate consequence of this condition is that it blocks the multiple S-adjunction found in (30b), but allows, and in fact requires, the structure in (31), in which one NP has been adjoined to S, the other to NP. In fact, more generally the adjunction constraint rules out the sort of representation for multiple quantification that we have been assuming, in which there is more than a single adjunction to S, a consequence that follows neither from Subjacency nor from the ECP. What is allowed is a structure akin to that for inverse linking, involving adjunction to NP, so that now multiple quantification sentences would have LF-representations of the form shown in (53):

(53)

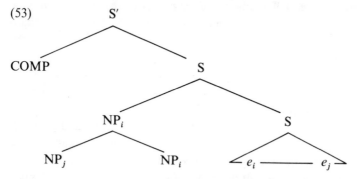

Here only a single operator is adjoined to S; the other is adjoined to this S-adjoined NP. In this structure the Scope Principle is just as much satisfied as in the multiple S-adjunction structure. Since S' remains the sole maximal projection dominating both NP_i and NP_j and there is no projection boundary between them (NP_j being contained within NP_i), these phrases govern each other. Moreover, their c-command, and hence scope, properties will be the same, the domain of each phrase being fixed at S'. Note that the ECP requires that the subject phrase be the one adjoined to S, since NP_j, adjoined to NP_i, does not govern outside of NP_i, because of the intervention of the latter projection's boundary. Thus, if the positions of NP_i and NP_j were reversed, an ECP violation would result, simply because of the failure of government. Thus, we no longer need refer to structural adjacency for the coindexing clause of the ECP in its application to structures of multiple quantification.

Now consider the following. Although broad scope of the *every*-phrase over *when* is a possible construal of *When did everyone see someone*, it apparently is barred in *When did someone see everyone*, even though in the absence of the *wh*-phrase the quantifiers can freely vary in scope, in either case. In the case at hand involving quantifier-*wh* interaction, this means that NP_j in (53) must have scope narrower than a phrase in COMP, although NP_i can have scope broader. This is because only the higher phrase, the one adjoined to S, satisfies the Scope Principle with respect to the phrase in COMP; government is blocked for the NP-adjoined phrase because of the intervention of a maximal projection boundary. Consequently, the universal phrase can interact scopally with the *wh*-phrase *when* in COMP only when it occurs in subject position, but not when it occurs in object position. Interestingly, though, this is not so when the subject phrase is not quantificational, so that a broad scope interpretation for the object NP is possible in *When did John see everyone*. This is as expected, because now *everyone* will be adjoined directly to S and can interact with the *wh*-phrase. Note that the latter contrast reinforces the notion that quantified and nonquantified expressions differ in their logical syntax, only the former undergoing LF-movement.[19]

The adjunction constraint is *not* an island constraint—it does not disallow extractions via LF-movement from island environments, so long as there is a valid adjunction site outside the island. Consequently, there is no bar to extracting QP from NP in result-clause constructions, and although (31) involves adjunction to NP, and not extraction, this is because S is the only node to which the other quantified NP could be adjoined. Extraction from NP is found, however, in the multiple *wh*-structure (52), which finds a quantificational analogue in the LF-representation of *Some student will investigate two dialects of every language*, which in turn admits of an interpretation in which the *every*-phrase has maximally broad scope, and the *some*-phrase intermediate scope. The structure giving rise to this construal is depicted in (54):

(54) $[_s[_{NP}$ every language$_2$ $[_{NP}$ some student]]$_3$ $[_s$ e_3 $[_{VP}[_{NP}$ two dialects of $e_2]_4$ $[_{VP}$ will investigate $e_4]]]]$

In this structure the quantified phrases govern one another, as described above; hence, the *every*-phrase can have broader scope. Moreover, both quantified phrases will have scope broader than the numerical phrase, which is adjoined to VP, thus taking narrowest scope.

A further case demonstrating the utility of the sort of NP-adjunction structures we have been considering arises in the analysis of the asymmetries of multiple *wh*-constructions, the so-called superiority effects. As discussed in chapter 2, this phenomenon can be taken as a consequence of the ECP. On this view (55a), the LF-representation of *What did who see*, was taken to contrast with (55b), the structure of *Who saw what*, since in the former the presence of *what* blocks proper government of the trace of *who*:

(55)a. $[_{s'}$ who$_3$ what$_2$ $[_s$ e_3 saw $e_2]]$
    b. $[_{s'}$ what$_2$ who$_3$ $[_s$ e_3 saw $e_2]]$

In discussing these examples, I glossed over the reasons for a particular point in this analysis: Why is the *wh*-phrase moved to COMP in LF placed to the left of the phrase already residing in COMP? Presumably such movement should be unconstrained, if we are to keep to our assumption that LF-movement is effectively free. But if this were so, and the LF-moved *wh*-phrase were placed to the right, then there would be no lack of proper government, for the subject empty category would now be bound by an immediately adjacent operator. Notice as well that the representations in (55) also seem to involve multiply filling COMP, a circumstance that is usually thought to be proscribed.

On the analysis developed in this section, however, these problems are resolved by assuming that additional movements to a filled COMP adjoin to the phrase already in COMP. This will then simply constitute another case of adjunction to NP. On this view the proper LF-representation of *Who admires what* will be (56):[20]

(56) *Who admires what?*

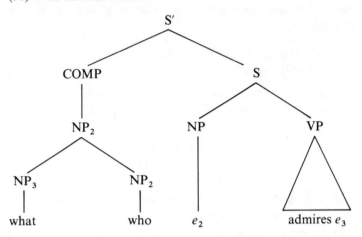

Since what is involved in deriving (56) is adjunction to a phrase in COMP, the latter position is not multiply filled. Rather, more than one phrase can be "in" COMP at LF because of the more general properties of movement onto this level; multiple movement to COMP is simply availing itself of the independent possibility of adjunction to NP in this case. Moreover, such structures will satisfy the *Wh*-Criterion of chapter 1, since both *wh*-phrases are dominated by COMP, although we will still be able to recognize which phrase is the "head" of COMP at LF: simply that phrase which is immediately dominated by COMP. In English this will be that (one) phrase which has been moved to that position in S-Structure, although not in languages such as Chinese, which, unlike English, require only that [+WH] COMPs be filled at LF. As for c-command relations in such structures, they will be the same as for other cases of NP-adjunction. That is, both NP_2 and NP_3 have S′ as their c-command domain and hence c-command their respective traces. In the case of NP_3 this is because it is dominated not by the NP_2-projection but by one of its member nodes; thus, S′ is the only maximal projection that dominates it. This will be so as well for further adjuncts to NP, as shown schematically in (57):

(57)

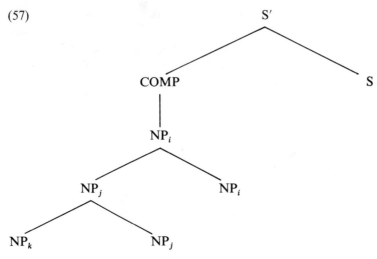

Here the further adjunct NP_k also has S' as its c-command domain; neither the NP_i nor the NP_j projections dominate it. As before, only one member of each projection dominates NP_k. Moreover, none of the adjuncts to NP in COMP will govern any A-position in S; this is possible exclusively for the phrase moved initially into COMP. This is because government will always be blocked by the occurrence of an NP boundary. Also, notice that the same c-command and government relations will be found if NP_k is adjoined to NP_i rather than NP_j, and that linear order of the phrases is irrelevant to these relations, as in (56), regardless of which projection it is adjoined to. Of course, further adjunctions will have exactly the same effects on c-command domain.[21]

The sort of COMP structure I have argued for at LF is also found in S-Structure in certain languages, such as Czech and Polish, which allow multiple fronting of wh-phrases at S-Structure. Example (58) is drawn from Toman's (1981) discussion of this phenomenon in Czech:

(58) Reknete nam, kdy co   kdo komu   dal.
     tell   us   when what who to whom gave
     'Tell us who gave what to whom when.'

The simplest assumption here is that COMP itself contains just one of the wh-phrases, and that the remainder are successively adjoined to it. Toman points out that the order of the wh-phrases in (58) is free. This is not surprising, though; all that is required is that the subject wh-phrase kdo be the head of COMP. So long as successive wh-phrases are adjoined to NPs in COMP so that a well-formed structure is derived, their linear order (or for that matter which particular NP in COMP they adjoin to) is immaterial.

Now given the LF-structure for multiple *wh*-questions being assumed here, the basic superiority effects—the difference between *Who admires what* and *What does who admire*—fall out directly from the ECP. Compare (56), repeated here, with the structure assigned to the latter sentence at LF:

(56) *Who admires what?*

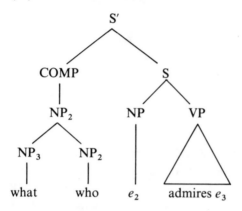

(59) **What does who admire?*

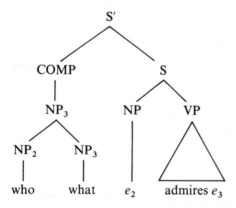

In these structures matters reduce immediately to proper government; thus, in (59) a maximal projection boundary, that of NP_3, intervenes between *who* and its trace; in (56), however, there is no intervening projection, and hence NP_2 properly governs its trace. This follows regardless of linear order. If NP_2 were adjoined to the right in (59), it would still be adjoined *within* the latter projection's boundary, and the resulting structure would just as well violate the ECP. The same holds for (56), except that here linear order would not disturb the existence of proper government.

Thus, assuming that multiple interrogation involves adjunction to the head *wh*-phrase moved into COMP at S-Structure allows us to ascribe basic superiority effects directly to lack of government, and hence to a violation of the ECP. As we shall see in chapter 5, assuming this sort of structure has a wide variety of other consequences, but under somewhat different assumptions regarding the basic constraints on well-formedness of structures at Logical Form.

Chapter 4
Branching, Lowering, and Extraposition

Independent Interpretations

The system of interpretation incorporating the Scope Principle formulated in chapter 2 admits two types of interpretations for multiple quantifiers: dependent and independent. Thus far we have not been concerned with the latter type, and for a very simple reason: the independent construal has in each case been first-order equivalent to a dependent construal. Since the Scope Principle applies only to *sequences* of quantifiers, if the independent interpretation is taken, each quantifier in the sequence must be interpreted independently of each of the others. Using the "branching quantifiers" notation of Hintikka (1974), such a sequence will have the representation shown in (1):

(1)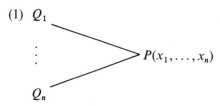

This will be equivalent, for the standard quantifiers, to some "linear" first-order formula (2):

(2) $Q_1, \ldots, Q_n \, P(x_1, \ldots, x_n)$

So, for instance, the independent interpretation of the sentence *Everyone admires someone*, given in symbols in (3), is logically equivalent to the linear structure in (4):

(3)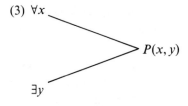

(4) $\exists y \, \forall x \, P \, (x, y)$

When we turn our attention to other quantifiers, however, such equivalences do not always hold; that is, we can find interpretations in which the valuation of neither quantifier is a function of the other. Barwise (1979) points out that the independent interpretation of multiple quantification sentences with nonstandard quantifiers like *most* or *more* will be logically distinct from any dependent interpretation, so long as all the quantifiers are either monotone increasing or monotone decreasing; he cites examples like *Most students admire most professors*. The two interpretations are also nonequivalent in sentences containing negative quantifiers, such as *Nobody loves nobody*. As discussed in chapter 1, such sentences are ambiguous between two logically independent linear interpretations; thus, *Nobody loves nobody* can be taken to mean either that everyone is a lover or that everyone is loved. Taking *no* to be logically glossed as the negated existential, the reason for this is apparent upon consideration of the formulae in (5), given the interdefinability of quantifiers and negation:

(5)a. $-\exists x \, -\exists y \, \text{loves}(x, y) \leftrightarrow \forall x \, \exists y \, \text{loves}(x, y)$ (Everyone is a lover)

   b. $-\exists y \, -\exists x \, \text{loves}(x, y) \leftrightarrow \forall y \, \exists x \, \text{loves}(x, y)$ (Everyone is loved)

This sentence also admits a further interpretation, on which no one is either loved or a lover, an interpretation that is logically distinct from the other two. But this construal is just the independent interpretation of this sentence, which can be represented in symbols as in (6);[1] again the negative quantifier has been glossed as a negated existential:

(6) $-\exists x$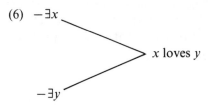

Loosely, (6) expresses that there are no x's or y's such that one loves the other; that is, no one is either a lover or loved. Here, since no scope relation holds between the quantifiers, there can be no interaction between the negations of the sort that gives rise to the universal import found with the dependent construals.

The independent interpretation is distinct in multiple numerical sentences like *Three directors have made five movies*. On the one hand, this sentence can be assigned two scopally interacting interpretations: either there are three directors, each of whom made five movies (broad scope for the subject phrase), or there are five movies, each of which was made by three directors (broad scope for the object phrase). Although on the former interpretation this sentence is compatible with there being fifteen movies, and on the latter with there being fifteen directors, it also has an interpretation on which it is compatible with neither of these circumstances; that is, its truth depends on there being just three directors and just five movies, such that the former made the latter. It is this construal—where there is no scope interaction between the numerical phrases—that is represened by the independent interpretation.[2]

To summarize, sentences with LF-representations containing a single sequence of quantifiers will be consistent with two types of interpretations; dependent or independent. The relations between the interpretations of a given token will be a matter of logic, so that the independent interpretation will be equivalent to a dependent interpretation in certain cases but not in others, depending upon the semantic properties of the particular quantifiers involved. Specifically, we have seen that when there are sequences containing standard quantifiers like *every* and *some*, there is a first-order equivalent. It turns out, however, that there are sequences containing such quantifiers that have been argued nonetheless to have distinct independent interpretations; these have been brought to light by Hintikka (1974). Hintikka points out that this will be so when the quantifiers are partially ordered, so that dependencies hold among the members of each branch, but not among quantifiers on distinct branches. This is shown graphically in (7), in which the interpretation of each Q_m^i, $(1 \leq m \leq n)$, will be a function of Q_{m-1}^i, but will be independent of the interpretation of any of the members of the Q^j branch. In this structure the quantifiers are "vertically" independent but "horizontally" dependent.

(7) $Q_1^i, \ldots, Q_n^i$

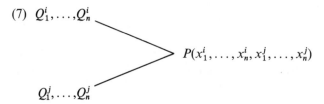

$$P(x_1^i, \ldots, x_n^i, x_1^j, \ldots, x_n^j)$$

$Q_1^j, \ldots, Q_n^j$

More concretely, Hintikka shows that a branching structure such as (8) has no first-order equivalent; its only linear equivalent is second-order, involving explicit quantification over functions, as shown in (9):

(8) $\forall x \, \exists y$

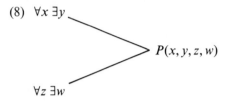

$P(x, y, z, w)$

$\forall z \, \exists w$

(9) $\exists f \, \exists g \, \forall x \, \forall z \, P(x, f(x), z, g(z))$

The latter formula expresses that the value of y is solely a function of x and that the value of w is solely a function of z; that is, the valuation of the narrow scope quantifiers on each branch of (8) is a function only of the other quantifier on its branch, being independent of the quantifiers on the other branch. The reason that (8) has no first-order equivalent is that this property cannot be represented in a first-order language, which lacks, so to speak, the ability to "comment" upon its own syntax.

Hintikka argues that these branching structures are in fact found in natural languages; among the examples he cites are those in (10), which are structurally paradigmatic of all his examples:

(10)a. Some relative of each villager and some relative of each towns-man hate each other.

b. Some book by every author is referred to in some essay by every critic.

Hintikka (1974, 167–168) describes the relevant semantic properties of these types of sentences with reference to example (10a) as follows:

Notice that in order for [(10a)] to be true, the relative of each townsman mentioned in it must not depend on the villager. In other words, [(10a)] need not be true in a situation described as follows.

The eldest relative of each villager and that relative of each townsman who is closest in age to the villager hate each other.

Yet in such a state of affairs a suitable linear-quantifier sentence . . . would be true. This example therefore serves to indicate why the linear-quantifier reading of [(10a)] will not quite do.

In surveying the examples Hintikka puts forth as exhibiting branching quantification, it is interesting that virtually every one involves complex noun phrases with inversely linked quantifiers. Is this an accidental choice of examples? I think not. Rather, we will find that it follows that just these contexts exhibit a logical syntax allowing for an independent interpretation. To see this, consider first the application of the Scope Principle to a simple inversely linked structure at LF, for example (11), repeated here from chapter 3:

(11)

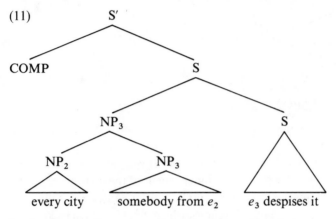

Reviewing the discussion of chapter 3, consider the structural relation of NP_2 and NP_3. They c-command one another, since S′ is the sole maximal projection dominating each, and there is no maximal projection boundary between NP_2 and NP_3, since the boundaries of the higher NP_3 projection are demarcated by its leftmost and rightmost brackets. The Scope Principle is therefore satisfied and, on the dependent interpretations, will give rise to the inversely linked and donkey interpretations, the latter just in case the conditions on pair quantifications are properly satisfied. But now consider the independent interpretation—that is, one that could be represented via branching—as in (12):

(12)   every city$_3$

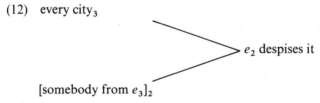

e_2 despises it

[somebody from e_3]$_2$

This structure, however, does not represent any determinate interpretation. This is because the quantifier on the higher branch cannot bind any variable; binding can be accomplished only if there is an interpretive dependency between the quantifiers. In conclusion, then, LF-representations like (11) admit only dependent interpretations, to the exclusion of the independent interpretation.

We are now in a position to consider examples such as those in (10). For illustration, consider the LF-representation assigned to (10b), *Some book by every author is referred to in some essay by every critic*:[3]

(13)

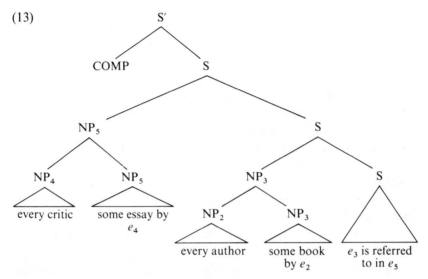

This structure is associated with a complex interpretation structure containing three Σ-sequences: $\{NP_2, NP_3\}$, $\{NP_4, NP_5\}$, $\{NP_3, NP_5\}$. The first two are satisfied only by dependent construals, as we have just seen. In fact, each can only have an inversely linked interpretation, with NP_2 and NP_4 having broad scope over NP_3 and NP_5, respectively, since the interpretive requirements for a donkey construal will not be met. Turning to the third sequence, consisting of NP_3 and NP_5, if they are construed independently, then we arrive directly at the branching construal described by Hintikka: there will be an interpretive dependency between NP_2 and NP_3, on the one hand, and NP_4 and NP_5, on the other, but each pair of quantifiers will be interpretively independent of the other pair. (13), then, is an LF-representation of the schematic form (7), one that displays partially ordered quantifiers and hence has no linear equivalent on this construal.[4]

I am claiming, then, that structures like (13) admit a construal in which the critic's essay is fixed independently of the author's book. What this comes down to is assigning the sequence made up of NP_3 and NP_5 an independent interpretation. But the Scope Principle also admits another type of interpretation, one in which these quantifiers are dependent, so that NP_3 has scope over NP_5 (or vice versa). That such linear interpretations exist is brought out by Hintikka, who points to the following example:

(14) The best-selling book by every author is referred to in the obituary essay on him by every critic.

To again cite Hintikka (p. 169), "The point is that in [(14)] the essay in question is not chosen on the basis of the critic alone, but also depends on the author in question." This circumstance obtains because the object NP contains a pronoun, bound as a variable by *every author*. But if (14) were assigned an independent construal, this would not be possible, for the pronoun and the quantifier would occur, so to speak, on independent branches and would not interpretively interact. This is not so, however, on the dependent interpretation, which is nonbranching and in which the phrase containing the pronoun will be dependent upon the phrase that binds it, by transitivity, as *the obituary essay on him* is dependent upon *the best-selling book*, which in turn is dependent upon *every author*. Since the pronoun will be within the c-command domain of the latter phrase at LF, only this type of construal will be compatible with taking the pronoun as a bound variable.

From our point of view the cases of branching quantifiers are interesting because, given our assumptions about the syntax of logical form, it is predictable that sentences of the particular syntactic construction under consideration will have a particular type of interpretation. Hintikka (1974), however, is concerned to draw a rather different moral. What he wishes to show is that, given that natural languages contain sentences whose semantic analysis involves branching quantifiers, and since such sentences have no first-order equivalents, one could conclude that natural language quantification cannot be captured by a first-order theory. For Hintikka the higher-order interpretation is what is *expressed* by sentences like those in (10). But one can view this in a rather different light, understanding formulas such as (9) instead as descriptions of the application of rules of quantifier interpretation (i.e., quantifications) to LF-representations of a certain form. In a sense the higher-order formula (9) is a comment on the syntax of branching quantifiers, asserting no more than that there are (interpretive) rules that apply in a certain way to given sentences; to say that this is expressed by a sentence would be like saying that *Who does Philby suspect* expresses that *wh*-movement applies to it. Insofar as such statements have status within the theory, they are perhaps akin to the ordering statements on rules in early versions of transformational grammar. But in general we do not wish to say that each sentence in some way marks which rules apply to it, or how they apply; this is just as true for semantic rules as for syntactic rules. Rather, as a point of methodology, we wish to see whether the relevant properties can be extracted to the level of general principle or rule. But this is just what we have done for branching quantifiers; given the syntactic constraints on representations at LF it simply follows, as a fact of logical syntax, that there will be only a partial ordering of the quantifiers for the relevant sentences. All that the analysis of branching quantifier sentences commits us to is that there are syntactic and semantic rules—which, after all, are functions of a particular kind—and principles, and it is these rules and principles that afford an account of the pertinent observations.

To continue, Barwise (1979) argues that Hintikka's examples, such as (10a), *Some relative of each villager and some relative of each townsman hate each other*, are also consistent with a weaker interpretation, which does not require that the choice of the villager's relative be independent of the choice of the townsman's. Rather, on this construal, the choice of villager's relative depends also on the choice of townsman, and inversely, the choice of townsman's relative on the villager. Barwise shows this by demonstrating the truth of (10a) in a model in which each villager is paired with a unique townsman and, in turn, each townsman is paired with a unique villager, such that neither hates the other. Then it is not the case that random choice of villager and townsman will guarantee that they hate each other. Barwise represents this schematically as in (15), with the universal quantifiers corresponding to the *each*-phrases, the existentials to the *some*-phrases:

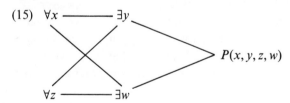

(15)

Barwise calls this "inessential" branching, since unlike a true branching construal it has linear, first-order equivalents:

(16) $\forall x \, \forall z \, \exists y \, \exists w \, P(x, y, z, w)$

How is this sort of interpretation to be accounted for?

Recall that a sentence can be assigned *any* interpretation so long as that interpretation is not inconsistent with the specifications of the interpretation structure projected from its LF-representation. More particularly, what is required for quantifiers is that whatever scope relations are specified by the associated Σ-sequences be satisfied. When we are dealing with a structure with just one Σ-sequence, this proposal is exactly what we have been maintaining all along; thus, a simple transitive clause can be assigned independent interpretations, whereas one associated with an inversely linked structure can only be assigned dependent interpretations. Now the sorts of branching structures we have been considering are each associated with three Σ-sequences of quantifiers, one of the former type and two of the latter. For the structure in (13), which in the relevant respects will be the same as that assigned to (10a), this means the sequences $\{NP_2, NP_3\}$, $\{NP_4, NP_5\}$, $\{NP_3, NP_5\}$. The claim is that any interpretation can be assigned consistent with the scope possibilities of these sequences; we have already seen that this is so for the branching interpretation in which the first two sequences have dependent interpretations and the latter an independent interpretation. Now consider (15). It also satisfies the strictures—just as with the "essential" branching interpretation, there is a dependency among members of each branch, but no dependency between the branches. But the Σ-sequences with which (15) is associated say nothing about interbranch connections; they are neutral on this. Thus, having the sort of dependencies depicted in (15) is perfectly well-formed; it is, so to speak, a free option of interpretation.

It is interesting to note that the linear equivalent of (15), namely (16), is also consistent with an interpretation of the quantifier sequences associated with (13), except that in this case all of the sequences are assigned dependent interpretations. Suppose for discussion that NP_3 has scope over NP_5 and, as before, that NP_2 has scope over NP_3 and NP_4 has scope over NP_5. Notice, however, that none of the sequences specifies the scope order of NP_4 with respect to NP_3. We may therefore take the phrase *each townsman* as having broader scope than *some relative ...*, that is, as having the interpretation represented by (16), as a linear, first-order interpretation of (10a).

To summarize: When we find multiple occurrences of inversely linked quantifiers, the independent construal permitted under the Scope Principle will lead to "branching" interpretations, as well as "linear" interpretations, and although the former entails the latter, they are not equivalent. Notice that the system developed here *predicts* that there will be a distinct independent interpretation in a particular sort of construction, those containing multiple occurrences of inversely linked quantifiers. An independent interpretation in this case will turn fundamentally on structural properties, since the quantifiers involved would not otherwise give rise to branching in other syntactic configurations. The relevant structural dimension is that with inversely linked quantifiers, the broad scope, NP-adjoined quantifier will be required to bear certain interpretive relations to the quantifier phrase to which it is adjoined. And in this regard we can take the syntactic properties of representations at LF as determining the range of interpretations available in natural languages.

Ambiguities of Lowering

In our discussions to this point we have been exploring the notion that the possibilities of LF-movement are rather free, at least insofar as they can effect adjunctions to any phrasal or clausal node. The class of structures so derived, however, is not equivalent to the class of structures generated by the grammar at LF. Rather, the latter class is a function of intersecting the possibilities of derivation with constraints limiting the liberty of such movements. Indeed, it is at this intersection that the ultimate empirical content of this theory of logical form lies. On this view, explanation ultimately resides not solely with the rules mapping onto LF per se, but rather in the interaction of these rules with the principles determining the well-formedness of syntactic representations at this level.

In chapter 2, in the context of the scope interactions of *wh*-phrases and quantifier phrases, we established that quantified phrases may be extracted from embedded domains; thus, we found an ambiguity in sentences such as *Who do you think everyone saw at the rally*, which is possible only if the complement subject can be adjoined to the matrix. Given our hypothesis about the freedom of movement, that this is possible is not surprising, although again the class of structures that can be generated is limited by general conditions. Thus, *Who thinks everyone saw you at the rally* is unambiguous, a function of the ECP. Now it turns out that there are also sentences in which the obverse circumstance is observed; that is, sentences in which a quantified phrase in a matrix clause can be "lowered" so as to find its scope within the complement. Thus, consider the following example, which displays a certain ambiguity of scope:

(17) A hippogryph is likely to be apprehended.

As discussed in May (1977, 1983), there is a construal of (17) under which it has the same truth-conditions as (18) (abstracting away from the effects of tense):

(18) It is likely that a hippogryph will be apprehended.

On this interpretation, (17) can be truthfully uttered without any supposition regarding the existence of hippogryphs. This contrasts with another construal under which it could not be truthfully uttered without this supposition. This ambiguity is quite general, found not only with raising adjectives but also with raising verbs like *seem* and *appear* and raising passives like *be believed* and *be expected*.

Now the contexts in which this ambiguity is found are rather limited; in fact, it is found just in "raising" constructions. Notice that active *believe* (as well as active *expect*) differs from its passive counterpart in being unambiguous; thus, we can construct minimally contrasting pairs of the following sort:

(19)a. No agent believes Philby to be a spy for the other side.
   b. No agent is believed by Philby to be a spy for the other side.

(19a) is unambiguous; it can only be understood as a denial of belief. (19b) can be construed this way as well, but it can also be understood as an assertion of a belief, namely, that there are no agents who are spies. That the existence of the ambiguity in question is somehow tied to properties of raising constructions can be easily observed. For one thing, the ambiguity is not found if the quantified phrase is not the raised subject; (19b) and (20) are a minimal pair:

(20) Philby is believed by no agent to be a spy for the other side.

(20) can only be understood as denying that there are beliefs that Philby is a spy for the other side. Second, the characteristic ambiguity that we observe with raising constructions is not found with control structures; (21) contrasts with (17):

(21) A hippogryph is anxious to be apprehended.

This sentence is unambiguous; its truth entails the existence of hippogryphs. It has no construal on which this is not so. Again this observation is quite general; none of the following display the ambiguity found in (17) and (19b):

(22)a. Some agent tried to be a spy for the other side.
   b. Some agent promised Philby to be a spy for the other side.
   c. Philby persuaded some agent to be a spy for the other side.
   d. Some agent wondered whether to be a spy for the other side.

Only in raising constructions, then, can quantified phrases standing as S-Structure matrix constituents be understood as being inside or outside the scope of the matrix predicate. In all other cases, only the latter construal is available. How is this observation to be accounted for?

To begin, consider the analysis of the ambiguous *A hippogryph is likely to be apprehended*. Recall our hypothesis that LF-movements are instances of "Move α," and thus that their application is free, in the sense that derivationally a moved phrase may be adjoined to any S node. In particular, there is nothing to prevent the derivation of (23b) alongside (23a); the former is derived by "raising" the S-Structure matrix subject to the matrix S, the latter by "lowering" it to the complement S:

(23)a. a hippogryph$_2$ [e_2 is likely [e_2 to be apprehended]]
    b. e_2 is likely [a hippogryph$_2$ [e_2 to be apprehended]]

It is apparent that the structures in (23) represent the relevant ambiguity, at least as far as scope of quantification is concerned. In (23a) the quantified phrase stands outside the scope of the matrix predicate *likely*; in (23b) it is inside the predicate's scope. But these structures differ in that (23b), in contrast to (23a), contains an empty category that is not c-commanded by a binding phrase. As discussed in chapter 1, however, unbound traces are normally proscribed at LF; still, if the structures in (23) are to represent the scope ambiguity of (17) properly, then it must be that both are well-formed at LF. Is there some principled reason, then, that "lowering" of a quantified phrase gives rise to a well-formed representation in just this case? Notice that a comparable representation for the parallel control sentence, *A hippogryph is anxious to be apprehended*, should not be well-formed, for in this sentence the quantified phrase is unambiguously understood as having broad scope.

In providing an answer, it is important to clarify matters in two interconnected areas. The first pertains to argument structure, the latter to the classification of empty categories. As we shall see, once we have fixed certain differences in raising and control structures with respect to the former, and intersected that with the properties of the latter, the differences of scope in these two constructions will simply follow as a consequence, provided that LF-movement is derivationally nonrestricted.

First, consider the properties of argument structure. As discussed in chapter 1, I take it, following Chomsky (1981), that the relation of lexical argument phrases to their structural manifestations in argument positions of predicates is mediated by the θ-Criterion:

(24) θ-Criterion
    a. Every θ-role must be assigned to just one argument chain.
    b. Every argument chain must be assigned just one θ-role.

The θ-roles characterize the argument positions of a predicate. Such positions must be properly related to argument chains, sequences of lexical (for instance, proper names) or nonlexical (for instance, traces functioning as variables) arguments. There are also lexical nonarguments, expletive *it* and *there*, whose occurrence is restricted to nonthematic positions. Thus, the subject position of a predicate that allows raising can be filled by an expletive element, but not the subject position of a control predicate:

(25)a. It is likely that Philby is a spy.
   b. *It is anxious that Philby is a spy.

This is a sufficient criterion on which to conclude that the subject positions of raising predicates are not θ-positions, an observation that melds with their semantic role as one-place predicates of clauses. It is also crucial to the fact that they allow movement to the matrix subject position from the complement subject, since the θ-Criterion proscribes a chain from being associated with two thematic positions. Thus, in the representation of *Philby is likely to be a spy*, *Philby* and its trace constitute an argument chain that is associated with only one thematic position—the one occupied by the trace—the position of the lexical NP being nonthematic.

As noted, variables, one type of empty category, are arguments from the perspective of the θ-Criterion. Since variables do not exhaust the types of empty categories, however, we need at this point to consider these elements in general. Following the system outlined in Chomsky (1982), we partition the empty categories by the features [±anaphor, ±pronominal], where each type of category will be associated with particular contextual properties. I have been presuming this kind of approach so far, taking variables, which will have the features [−anaphor, −pronominal], to be empty categories in A-positions that are $\bar{\text{A}}$-bound. Empty categories contained in A-positions that are A-bound are anaphors; that is, they have the feature specification [+anaphor, −pronominal]. The distribution of the latter category is in part accounted for by the constraints on syntactic "opacity" effects also found with overt anaphors (cf. condition A of the binding theory of Chomsky (1981)). Both types of empty categories are found in (26):

(26) who$_2$ [e_2 is likely [e_2 to be a spy]]

Here the *wh*-phrase in COMP $\bar{\text{A}}$-binds the left-hand trace, a variable, which in turn binds the right-hand trace, an anaphor, arising from NP-movement.

A third type of empty category has the features [+anaphor, +pronominal]; this is what has been called PRO. The defining property of its distribution is that it occurs only in ungoverned positions, so it is found as the embedded subject in control constructions, such as those in (22) (cf. Chomsky (1981)). PRO may be free—that is, not c-commanded by any antecedent—as in *PRO eating sushi is a way of life in Japan*, but if it is bound, it is bound by a category in a thematic position. In this regard control structures—in which the empty category and its antecedent, if any, are base-generated—differ from raising structures, which involve movement, in that the A-binder in the latter occurs in a nonthematic position.

The fourth type of empty category has the features [−anaphor, +pronominal]; that is, it is an empty pronominal. Chomsky (1982) has proposed that there are two types of such pronominals, referential and expletive, mirroring the types of overt pronouns. Such categories are hypothesized to differ from the pronominal anaphor PRO in occurring in governed positions, though they resemble it in being able to occur free in these positions. Empty pronominals are most clearly found in "pro-drop" languages, in which the referential empty pronominal has been argued to occur when the subject is lexically absent, the expletive empty pronominal when the subject has been inverted (see Chomsky (1982), Safir (1982), Jaeggli (1984), and discussion in chapter 5). In contrast to languages like Italian and Spanish, English lacks any referential empty pronominal, but, as we shall see, it does countenance empty expletives, nonlexical counterparts of the expletive *it*. Like its lexical counterpart, the empty expletive will be nonthematic and will lack agreement features; note the ungrammaticality of *It seems to itself that Philby is discreet* as opposed to *Philby seemed to himself to be discreet*. Moreover, given that such categories exist, it can be shown that they cannot occur in ungoverned contexts, and hence that they must be distinct from PRO, as Safir (1982) has illustrated on the basis of examples of the following sort:

(27) *To seem that John will be elected by a majority is surprising.

For a detailed discussion of the properties of expletive empty categories, see Safir (1982).

To summarize, the empty categories occurring in A-positions can be classified on the basis of the features [±pronominal, ±anaphor]. Variables, which must be Ā-bound, are [−pronominal, −anaphor]; anaphors, which must be A-bound, are [−pronominal, +anaphor]. Both types of categories must occur in governed positions. In contrast, PRO, with the features [+pronominal, +anaphor], is restricted to ungoverned positions. Its occurrence may be either bound or free. Free occurrence, however, is required for the expletive empty category, which is [+pronominal, −anaphor]. It is like variables and anaphors in occurring in governed positions, but unlike them in being a nonargument and therefore being restricted to nonthematic positions.

We can now reconsider the well-formedness of the LF-representations of the ambiguous *A hippogryph is likely to be apprehended*, repeated here:

(23)a. a hippogryph$_2$ [e_2 is likely [e_2 to be apprehended]]
   b. e_2 is likely [a hippogryph$_2$ [e_2 to be apprehended]]

Recall that in (23a) the quantified phrase stands outside the scope of the matrix predicate *likely*, from which it Ā-binds the matrix subject, a variable. The latter category in turn A-binds the complement subject, which is an anaphor. In this respect (23a) is no different than (26). In (23b), on the other hand, *a hippogryph* is inside the scope of *likely*. Notice that in this structure the status of the lower trace will be changed after lowering. No longer will it be an anaphor, an A-bound trace; instead, it will be a variable, since its most local binder is an Ā-binding operator. At LF, then, its status, though changed from that in (23a), is without flaw.

(23b), however, contains a second empty category to be accounted for: namely, the matrix subject position vacated by lowering the quantified phrase. What is its status? First, it is free; hence, it cannot qualify as either a variable or an anaphor. Consequently, if it is anything, it must be either PRO or an expletive, since these are the categories that can occur free. It cannot be the former, however, since the matrix subject position in (23b) is governed, being the subject of a tensed clause. Therefore, this category can only be expletive, and indeed it satisfies all the criteria of this category. Not only is this a governed, free position; it is also nonthematic.[5] We may conclude, then, that given the characterization of empty categories, this structure is also well-formed, representing the narrow scope construal. The analysis can be extended to more complex examples involving greater levels of embedding of raising predicates. In such structures any of the intermediate traces can serve as a variable or can be expletive, depending upon which S the lowered phrase is adjoined to, giving rise to a correspondingly greater degree of ambiguity. So, for instance, *A unicorn is believed to be likely to be apprehended* is three ways ambiguous, only one of the three interpretations entailing that there are unicorns.[6]

In chapter 3 I proposed that if an operator in an Ā-position c-commands a predicate, then it must c-command all the arguments of that predicate. Raising constructions are parallel to exceptional Case-marking constructions in taking S-complements. In the terminology of Chomsky (1981) they are also "S'-deletion" predicates, differing from verbs like *believe* in not assigning Case, so that although they govern their complement's subject, this category must be lexically empty. Now, as we have just seen, narrow scope for a quantified phrase is possible in raising constructions. This is represented by adjunction to the complement S, a position from which the c-command domain of the adjoined phrase extends to include the higher predicate. In doing so, however, it will also c-command *all* the arguments of this predicate, since raising predicates do not have subject arguments; instead, the [NP, S] position is nonthematic. Thus, the fact that the lowered phrase fails to c-command the matrix subject is inconsequential.

I am claiming, then, that the representation (23b) will be nondistinct at LF (again, modulo tense) from that of (18). Both will contain "sentential operators" with expletive subjects, taking a single sentential argument. The theory will allow this type of structure to arise either by base-generation or derivationally via LF-movement. In the latter case, the greater freedom of such movements to structurally "downgrade" phrases gives a salutary result. But, as pointed out in chapter 1, not just any matrix subject can take narrow scope. It is absent in the simplest sort of example; for instance, *No agent believes Philby to be/is a spy for the other side* precludes any construal with the quantifier inside the scope of *believe*. This stems from the matrix subject in these examples being thematic. Hence, if an empty category is to occur in this position at LF, it must be one that can bear a θ-role. On the one hand, it can be a variable, which will arise if the subject phrase is adjoined to the matrix S. On the other hand, if this phrase were lowered, the resulting empty category would be free, and the only empty category that can occur free and bear a θ-role is PRO. But the subject position of active *believe* is a governed position, and therefore PRO is excluded. If *believe* is passivized, however, its syntactic properties become nondistinct from those of a raising predicate; in particular, its subject is nonthematic, as the occurrence of the expletive subject in *It was believed that Philby was a spy for the other side* attests. This allows us to account for the contrast in (19), because now, when the subject phrase is lowered in deriving an LF-representation for *No agent is believed by Philby to be a spy*, the resulting empty matrix subject will be the empty expletive, which, by definition, occurs in governed, nonthematic positions. This example in turn contrasts with (20), *Philby is believed by no agent to be a spy for the other side.* Although subject position is non-thematic, the position of the quantified phrase *no agent* is not. Lowering of this phrase, therefore, is also prohibited, since it would result in a category that could only be classified as PRO—since this is a thematic position—but is governed.

Finally, recall the contrast between (17) and (21): the control construction (21) differs from the raising construction (17) in not exhibiting the scope ambiguity we are considering, since it lacks the narrow scope construal. These examples differ structurally as follows:

(28)a. a hippogryph is likely [e to be apprehended]
    b. a hippogryph is anxious [PRO to be apprehended]

Both raising and control constructions contain bare infinitival complements, trace and PRO both being lexically empty categories, differing in that the former arises via movement, the latter by base-generation. Moreover, whereas the former category occurs in a governed position, the latter does not. In this regard raising constructions are like exceptional Case-marking constructions in taking S-complements, perhaps as a consequence of S′-deletion. Control and raising differ also, and for our purposes crucially, in that in control constructions the matrix subject is thematic. Thus, the matrix subject in a control construction may have a thematic role distinct from that of PRO, which it controls; for example, in *A hippogryph is anxious to roam free* the matrix subject is theme, and the complement subject is agent. Also, as noted above, such predicates disallow expletive *it* as subject: **It is anxious that a hippogryph be apprehended.* But given the thematic status of the subject, the semantic contrast between raising and control follows directly. Thus, consider the structures in (29):

(29)a. a hippogryph$_2$ [e_2 is anxious [e_2 to be apprehended]]
    b. e_2 is anxious [a hippogryph$_2$ [e_2 to be apprehended]]

Like (23a), (29a) is nonproblematic. The trace of LF-movement is a variable, and the embedded empty category is PRO. In (29b), in which the quantified phrase has been lowered, the complement subject is now Ā-bound, and hence a variable.[7] The problem here, however, is with the matrix category; it cannot be PRO, since this position is governed, nor can it be the empty expletive, since this is a thematic position. Thus, such structures are ruled out as ill-formed at LF, containing an undefined category. The range of interpretation of control constructions is therefore more narrowly limited, being comparable to that of structures with full clausal complements.[8]

A number of alternative analyses could be considered. For instance, rather than "lowering" the subject NP, the matrix predicate could be raised. The scope ambiguity would then depend upon whether the raised matrix subject NP was adjoined higher or lower than the moved predicate. There is evidence against this suggestion, however. First, it would not distinguish between different types of predicates. Why could only raising predicates be moved, and not others? After all, the scope ambiguity we are considering is characteristic of raising constructions. Perhaps a semantic generalization might be offered, for instance, that all the predicates concerned are, in some sense, modal. But this would fail to distinguish active and passive occurrences of *believe*; even if there were some generalization linking *believe* with predicates like *appear* and *likely*, we would have to ask why we find an ambiguity in *No agent is believed by Philby to be a spy for the other side* but none in *No agent believed Philby to be a spy for the other side*. Presumably both occurrences of *believe* mean the same thing, and thus both should undergo the putative predicate raising rule. Further, why wouldn't other matrix constituents interact scopally with the predicate? As pointed out, we only find ambiguities with respect to the subject NP; witness the nonambiguity of *Philby is believed by no agent to be a spy for the other side*. Finally, the proposed alternative would incorrectly predict the possibilities of anaphora in a sentence such as *No agent was believed by his superior to be a spy for the other side*. The relevant observation about this sentence is that when the matrix subject is understood with narrow scope, the pronoun cannot be taken as a bound variable, as in *It was believed by his superior that no agent was a spy for the other side*, which paraphrases it. On the account proposed here this follows directly, since when the subject NP is adjoined to the complement clause it no longer has any matrix constituents within its scope. It does not follow, however, on the proposed alternative. This is because the narrow scope interpretation of the quantifier is represented at LF with the matrix subject adjoined to the matrix S, just in a position lower than the moved predicate. But from this position it *includes* constituents of the matrix within its scope, so the pronoun should be interpretable as a bound variable. The point here is that anaphora varies as a function of the scope of the raised phrase, and only on an analysis in which the alternative scopes are represented by adjunction to the matrix or complement clauses will this interaction be properly accounted for.

Boundedness of Extraposition

To this point our considerations of the structure of LF-representations have centered around what, intuitively, are "semantic" phenomena, primarily the relative scope of quantifiers. But there is no reason to think that our notions of logical syntax will be relevant to the explanation of just this kind of phenomena; rather, given that LF is a level of syntactic representation, it is to be expected that it will also play a role in accounting for phenomena that have been traditionally thought of as "syntactic." In this section we will treat such a case, where the greater level of structural articulation at LF affords a natural explanation that would not otherwise be available. We will see that what appears to be a constraint on extractability of movement onto S-Structure is in fact a constraint on the extractability of quantified phrases at LF.

The phenomenon in question is the "Right-Roof Constraint," first discussed in Ross (1967). Ross observed that extraposition from an NP within an embedded clause is "clause-bound," as can be illustrated by the necessity of disjoint reference between the italicized phrases in (30):

(30) *I told *her* that the concert was attended by many people last year who made *Mary* nervous.

Thus, if the extraposed clause is attached to the complement clause, it will be c-commanded by the matrix object, but this would not be so if it were adjoined to the matrix. And, as is well known, disjoint reference is required when a pronoun c-commands its antecedent (Lasnik (1976), Reinhart (1976, 1983)); it follows that extraposition from NP must be constrained not to extract outside a clause of which the relative clause is an immediate constituent.

(30), however, contrasts with (31), in which there is also extraposition:

(31) I told *her* that the concert was attended by so many people last year that I made *Mary* nervous.

In this example, involving result-clause extraposition, disjoint reference is *not* required, and a conjoint interpretation is possible for the italicized elements. Thus, it would seem that in this case extraposition must be possible to the matrix, since only in this position will the pronoun not c-command its antecedent. The Right-Roof Constraint therefore does not hold of extraposition constructions generally, or so it would appear.

How can we characterize the properties of extraposition constructions so as to account for this contrast? The answer is to be found in the analysis of extraposition developed in Guéron and May (1984), from which the following discussion is drawn. The idea developed there is that the head of an extraposition construction must govern its extraposed complement at LF. To understand the content of this theory, consider the derivation of an extraposition-from-NP construction such as (32), with the S-Structure representation in (33), where the extraposed clause has been adjoined to S.[9]

(32) Many books have been published recently which I've enjoyed reading.

(33)

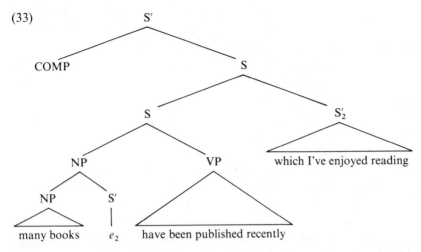

QR applies to the quantified head of the relative construction in this structure; indeed, it is a basic observation about extraposition from NP that it is from quantified heads. Note that the moved phrase will include the trace of the extraposed clause, since LF-movement pied pipes, as argued in chapter 1, giving the LF-representation (34):

(34)

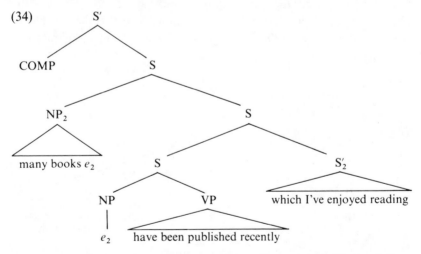

Now recall that a phrase A governs another phrase B only if A and B are dominated by all the same maximal projections and there is no maximal projection boundary between them. This is satisfied in (34) because S′, and only S', dominates the LF-moved head phrase and the S-Structure-moved extraposed clause, both of which are adjoined to S. Thus, via LF-movement the appropriate complementation relations have been reestablished at LF, so that the head and complement form a single operator at LF, just as they would if there had been no extraposition at all. Notice that the trace of S' contained in NP_2 is properly bound in this structure: it is c-commanded by the extraposed clause, since every maximal projection dominating the latter (i.e., S') also dominates the former.

The same constraint on complementation at LF must be satisfied in the case of result-clause extraposition, and this will be accomplished in the same fashion, via movement of the head of the construction. But there is a crucial difference between result-clause and extraposition-from-NP constructions. Whereas in the latter the head is an NP, in the former it is a QP, so that *so* is the head of the extraposed clause in (35), not the NP that contains it.

(35) So many books have been published recently that I haven't been able to read them all.

To derive the LF-representation of this sentence, QR will apply to its S-Structure representation, but will move only the QP *so*, since only this phrase constitutes the head of the construction. Note that there will be no pied piping here, since QP is categorially distinct from the phrase that contains it. This gives (36):

(36)

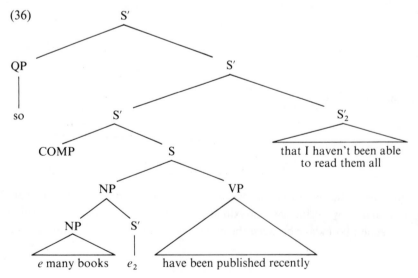

(37)

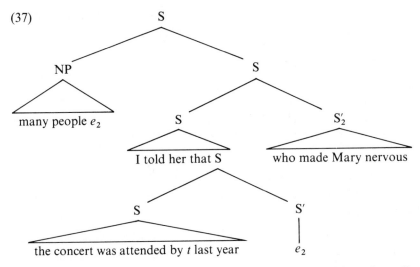

In this structure the extraposed clause has attained its position via cyclic movement, so there is a trace of S′, which occurs in an $\overline{A}$-position attached to the complement S. But whereas the extraposed clause itself, adjoined to the matrix, properly binds an empty category—the trace contained within the head phrase—the category adjoined to the complement S binds nothing at all. But then on the assumption that vacuous $\overline{A}$-binding is proscribed at LF—a natural assumption, really no more than the notion that vacuous operators are precluded at this level—(37) will be ruled out.[11] This accounts, then, for the Right-Roof Constraint—given the basic condition on government for extraposition, and given that LF-movement is an instance of "Move α" and hence obeys general conditions on movement, it follows directly that extraposition is clause-bound, since in those structures in which there is "broad scope," a category will occur illicitly in an $\overline{A}$-position.

The analysis just described predicts that if for some reason the extraposed clause need not gain its surface position by cyclic movements, then there should be no right-roof effect; that is, the extraposed clause will not have to be a constituent of the same clause at D-Structure and S-Structure (and, by extension, LF). This is, in fact, precisely what we find when there has been extraposition from an NP in COMP:

(38) Which spy does Angleton believe that Burgess recruited who ultimately became a mole?

In this case the entire wh-phrase *which spy who ultimately became a mole* was extracted to the matrix COMP from the embedded clause, followed by extraposition to the matrix S. (The head *wh*-phrase will govern the extra-posed clause since the matrix S′ is the only maximal projection dominating each.) But since this derivation does not involve cyclic extraposition, no offending empty category has been deposited of the sort giving rise to the ill-formedness of (37).

The final question which arises in this analysis is, why doesn't result-clause extraposition also obey the Right-Roof Constraint? That is, why is conjoint reference possible in (31), in contradistinction to (30)?

(30) *I told *her* that the concert was attended by many people last year who made *Mary* nervous.

(31) I told *her* that the concert was attended by so many people last year that I made *Mary* nervous

The answer lies in the fact that the head of the extraposed result clause is a QP, not an NP, which means that there is no pied piping under LF-movement. In particular, it means that at LF the trace of S′ within NP will remain in its S-Structure position, so that the LF-representation asso-ciated with (31), in which the result clause occurs attached to the matrix, is as follows:

(39)

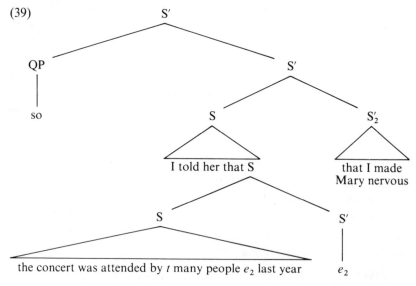

It has been assumed that in the derivation of this structure the extraposed clause has attained its S-Structure position via cyclic movements, a conse-quence of the Subjacency Condition. The significant difference between

this structure and (37) is that the cyclic, empty, $\bar{\text{A}}$-adjoined category that this sort of movement gives rise to does not vacuously bind; rather, it c-commands the trace of S′ that occurs in the embedded clause, and in turn is c-commanded by the extraposed result clause itself. Thus, this structure is well-formed, with QR deriving a structure in which a phrase has "broad scope."

In chapter 3 a condition was developed requiring that if an operator c-commands a predicate, then it must c-command all the arguments of that predicate. The requirement has at its foundation the notion that predicate-argument structure must be properly expressed at LF. As such it is intended to condition the occurrence of those operators that are "thematic," in the sense of binding variables that fill (or whose traces fill) argument positions; excluded from its purview, therefore, are any $\bar{\text{A}}$-adjoined elements that are not thematic in this sense. This predicts that if an operator were to bind a nonargument position, it could be adjoined to a complement S′ without running afoul of the stricture on binding of argument positions. Exactly this situation arises with result clauses; thus, in addition to the "broad scope" just described, they can also have "narrow scope." This is perhaps most clearly illustrated by the ambiguity of (40), between being a statement of Ehrlichman's belief in a causal relation and being a statement that Ehrlichman's belief is itself a causal agent (this ambiguity was originally brought to light by Liberman (1974)):

(40) Ehrlichman believed that Nixon was so crazy that he acted irrationally.

This ambiguity is to be represented by adjoining the result clause–QP pair either to the matrix or to the complement S′. Whereas the former construal will be represented as just described, the latter will be represented by (41):

(41) [$_{S'}$ Ehrlichman believed [$_{S'}$ so$_2$ [$_{S'}$ that Nixon was e_2 crazy] that he acted irrationally]]

But even though in (41) the $\bar{\text{A}}$-adjoined *so* c-commands the higher predicate *believe*, this does not lead to a contravention of the condition, since *so* is nonthematic in the requisite sense. Thus, such examples contrast with focus constructions, in which narrow scope is excluded, as described in chapter 3. This difference turns on the differential status vis-à-vis thematic argument structure of the constituents undergoing LF-movement in each of these constructions.

The analysis of the boundedness of extraposition extends to other domains; thus, although extraposition from NP is not possible from islands such as relative clauses, result-clause extraposition is. (42) therefore contrasts with the grammatical (43):

(42) *Several critics who have reviewed many books were at the party which I've enjoyed reading.
(43) Several critics who I have known for so long were at the party that I didn't bother to speak to them at all.

(42) can be ruled out the same way as (30); that is, even though the head phrase may be extracted from the relative clause, the cyclicity required by Subjacency for the extraposed clause will necessarily give rise to an offending vacuous operator. But in (43) no such problem arises, parallel to the analysis of (31). Notice, however, that it must be that Subjacency does not ordain any absolute restriction against extraction to the higher clause, or else the government condition could never be satisfied for the result-clause construction.

"Boundedness" effects are by no means the only aspect of extraposition constructions that can be argued to turn on the syntax of LF. Others include the occurrence of split antecedents with result-clause extraposition but not with extraposition from NP, which is a consequence of the distinctness of indices imposed by the θ-Criterion (chapter 1), and the restrictions on multiple extraposition, which follow from assuming that at LF multiple quantification is represented by successive adjunctions to NP, as described in chapter 3. See Guéron and May (1984) for detailed discussion of these and other properties of extraposition constructions. The case discussed here, however, is of particular interest in the current context because it illustrates how the theory of LF, in providing a degree of structural articulation not available at other levels of representation, affords an explanation in terms of independently motivated principles. In doing so, it relates prima facie syntactic phenomena to matters of a seemingly semantic nature, such as quantifier scope and the possibilities of quantifying in. Thus, the grammar freely permits quantifying in, in the sense that movement is free from the complement to the matrix clause (as this interacts with other aspects of LF-structure), but in some contexts certain constraints will be called into play, and these constraints may limit the well-formedness of the representations so derived. This is just what we have seen with the boundedness of extraposition. In the next chapter we will among other things continue to investigate conditions that will further constrain the well-formedness of "long-distance" movement in LF.

Chapter 5
Variables, Binding Paths, and Government

Problems with the ECP

So far we have been examining the consequences of conditions on the syntax of logical form, in particular, those that affect the well-formedness of structures representing quantification. The conditions in question have all had the property of making reference solely to formal, syntactic properties of logical representations, and it is through the applicability of such conditions that the range of interpretation of natural languages can be seen to be subject to grammatical determination. It is in this regard that there is content to logical syntax above and beyond being simply a mirror of semantic structure.

In this chapter I reconsider the condition that in the course of the previous chapters has emerged as one of the primary conditions on LF: the Empty Category Principle. The ECP encounters a number of problems, both empirical and conceptual, which when taken together indicate that it perhaps does not refer to exactly the right properties of LF-representations. What are these problems? One is that the ECP has not been applied in a uniform manner. Most of the cases we have considered have involved the "coindexing clause" of the ECP and have centered around the failure of proper government of an empty category in subject position, which obtains just when it is governed by a coindexed phrase. The lack of parallelism stems from the fact that in some cases—for instance, the purported violation arising from adjoining the quantified phrase to S in the LF-representation of *Who bought everything for Max*—the ECP is violated because a phrase is moved to a position that prevents a trace from being *adjacent* to the phrase with which is it coindexed (although structural government still obtains), whereas in others—in particular, with superiority violations like *What did who see*—the ECP is violated because of a failure of government. But although in the latter case, since LF-movement adjoined to NP in COMP, the boundary of the NP moved to COMP in S-Structure will block government (hence proper government), in the former case it is only a convention that QR is shown as effecting a left Chomsky-adjunction. A structure at LF with right adjunction would exhibit exactly the same structural properties relevant to scope and government, but now the phrase in COMP would be adjacent to its trace, which it would therefore properly govern.

Though such an asymmetry in and of itself may be of no great importance—it may simply indicate the need for a more precise characterization of the condition—its significance looms larger when taken in light of more specific empirical problems. For instance, LF-movements do seem to occur from positions in which proper government is held not to obtain. Consider the focus and result-clause constructions in (1) and (2):[1]

(1) Dean believed that whó had erased the White House tapes.
(2) I told her that so many people attended last year's concert that I made Mary nervous.

In (1) *who* is moved to the matrix S', as is *so* in (2), under the construal of this sentence in which the pronoun is interpreted conjointly with *Mary*. In both cases LF-movement extracts a phrase from a position immediately posterior to the complementizer *that*, a position from which movement is proscribed by the ECP. A non–properly governed subject of a tensed clause will also be found in the LF-representation of *A hippogryph is likely to be apprehended*, in which the subject NP is "lowered," giving rise to an empty expletive category. And why should this category escape the detrimental effects of the ECP?

Similarly, the ECP should distinguish the possible interpretations of *Who do you think that everyone saw at the rally* as opposed to *Who do you think everyone saw at the rally*, in which the complementizer is absent. Now the existence of an ambiguity in the latter sentence is predicated on the possibility of extracting the quantified phrase and adjoining it to the matrix S, a position in which it will govern the *wh*-phrase. But if the ECP were in effect, and if it applied to QR as it does to *wh*-movement (perhaps under the assumption that QR is cyclic), we would not expect this sort of movement to be possible for the former sentence, since this movement would give rise to a trace that is not properly governed. But this is contrary to fact, since both of these sentences are ambiguous.

Another problem arises in the case of superiority effects, namely, lack of generality. Though certain superiority effects can be accounted for directly by the ECP, as we have seen, others cannot be. Thus, (3a) contrasts with (3b), although both the trace of the S-Structure-moved *wh*-phrase and the trace of the LF-moved *wh*-phrase are properly governed positions:[2]

(3)a. ?Whom did you tell that Harry saw who?

b. *Who did you tell whom that Harry saw?

Problems also arise with adjunction-to-VP constructions; recall that this position is not c-commanded by V, and hence not properly governed, since the VP-projection dominates V but not phrases adjoined to VP. We appealed to this lack of government in accounting for the lack of *wh*-movement in presentational *there*-sentences. But there are cases in which movement is possible precisely from this position. Rizzi (1982) has pointed out that in Italian broad scope over the matrix clause is possible for the polarity item *nessuno* 'nobody' when it occurs as an inverted postverbal subject, adjoined to VP within the complement clause:

(4) Non pretendo che sia arrestato nessuno.
     neg require   that be arrested nobody
     'I do not require that nobody be arrested.'

Rizzi contrasts such examples with sentences like (5), for which he claims no broad scope construal is available:

(5) Non pretendo che nessuno ti   arresti.
     neg require   that nobody you arrest
     'I do not require that nobody arrest you.'

This difference can be explained, according to Rizzi, if extraction is possible from the postverbal subject position but blocked (presumably by the ECP) from the preverbal subject. Rizzi extends this point, proposing that long *wh*-movement of subjects in Italian, as in sentences like *Chi credi che verrà* 'Who do you believe (that) will come', involves a derivational step with a structure comparable to the S-Structure of (4). But if the VP-adjoined position is not properly governed, how can movement be possible from this position? Recall that there is evidence internal to Italian that this position is not c-commanded by V; this is what explained the absence of *ne*-cliticization in VP-adjoined subject inversion constructions. But if there is no c-command by V, then there is no government by V, and hence no proper government by V either.

Paths and Multiple Operators

Though all of these considerations could perhaps be explained away in some fashion consistent with the ECP, it is worthwhile to see if some other generalization might account more naturally for the full range of phenomena we have been investigating. As a point of departure, notice that most of the cases we have sought to subsume under the ECP have involved "interactive" effects. That is, when we have had recourse to the ECP—namely, in multiple quantification, multiple interrogation, and mixed quantification-interrogation constructions—it has been because assigning scope to one phrase has disturbed proper government of an empty category bound by another phrase. But perhaps it is not so much the effect on government that is important, but rather the relation of the "paths" of binding that the various movements onto LF give rise to. That such relations between phrases in $\overline{A}$-positions and the empty categories they bind are a determinant of syntactic well-formedness has been argued extensively by Pesetsky (1982), who suggests that structures involving multiple $\overline{A}$-bindings must satisfy what he calls the *Path Containment Condition* (PCC). It may be stated loosely as follows:

(6) Path Containment Condition

Intersecting $\overline{A}$-categorial paths must embed, not overlap.

A *path* is a set of occurrences of successively immediately dominating categorial nodes connecting a bindee to its binder.[3] Each contiguous pair of nodes within a path constitutes a *path segment*, and a path, more precisely, is just a set of such segments. I will refer to a set of such paths associated with an LF-representation as its *path structure*. Paths *intersect* only if they have a common path segment. Consequently, paths sharing a single node do not intersect. If the paths do intersect, then the PCC requires that one of the paths must properly contain all the members of the other.

Though the consequences of structural intersection vs. nesting have been discussed in a number of places, the particular interest in Pesetsky's formulation is its extension to a wide variety of seemingly disparate phenomena, including "*that*-trace" effects, the Subject Condition, across-the-board parallelisms, and the Coordinate Structure Constraint.[4] But rather than exploring the motivation for this condition, let us examine its application to the cases we have been concerned with. To see the effect of the PCC, consider the multiple quantification structures in (7) and (8); recall that the latter was purportedly ruled out by the ECP because the intervention of the NP_3 between NP_2 and its trace blocked proper government:

(7)

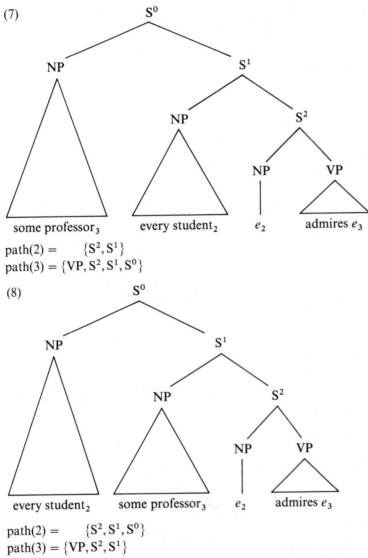

path(2) =   {S², S¹}
path(3) = {VP, S², S¹, S⁰}

(8)

path(2) =   {S², S¹, S⁰}
path(3) = {VP, S², S¹}

In each case the relevant categorial paths have been indicated. Notice that in (7) the nodes constituting path(2) between the subject empty category and the Ā-adjoined phrase *every student* are a proper subset of those making up path(3) between the object trace and *some professor*. On the other hand, such proper embedding is not found in (8), in which the intersecting paths overlap, so that neither is a proper subset of the other. It is the latter configuration that is ruled out by the PCC.

The analysis will be quite parallel for the sort of quantifier-*wh* constructions discussed in chapter 2. Thus, assuming adjunction to S for the
quantified phrase in each case, the LF-representations of *What did everyone
buy for Max* and *Who bought everything for Max* will contrast just as (7)
and (8) do:[5]

(9)

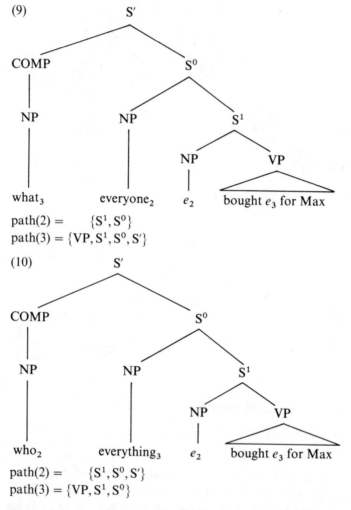

path(2) = $\{S^1, S^0\}$
path(3) = $\{VP, S^1, S^0, S'\}$

(10)

path(2) = $\{S^1, S^0, S'\}$
path(3) = $\{VP, S^1, S^0\}$

Again these contrast as desired; it is only when *wh*-movement has been
from object position that a well-formed LF-representation is derivable,
since it is only in (9) that the paths embed.[6] So it is only to *What did
everyone buy for Max* that an ambiguity can be attributed, since only this
sentence can be associated with an LF-representation in which government

holds between the operators. On the other hand, when there is adjunction to VP in the LF-representation of *Who bought everything for Max*, there is no violation of the PCC; in fact, the PCC is not even relevant to this structure, since none of its categorial paths intersect at all, as (11) shows:

(11)

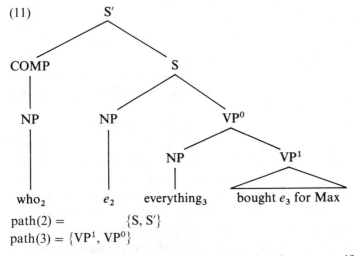

$$path(2) = \{S, S'\}$$
$$path(3) = \{VP^1, VP^0\}$$

The subject-object asymmetry found in the above quantifier-*wh* sentences is mirrored in the following pair, ambiguity being found only in the (a) sentence.

(12)a. Who do you think everyone saw at the rally?
    b. Who do you think saw everyone at the rally?

In order to derive a structure subject to the Scope Principle, it is necessary to move *everyone* to the matrix S; only in this position will it govern the *wh*-phrase. But this will only be possible, in a fashion consistent with the PCC, for (12a):

(13)a. $[_{S'}$ who$_2$ $[_S$ everyone$_3$ $[_S$ do you think $[_{S'}[_S$ e_3 saw e_2 at the rally]]]]]

   $$path(2) = \{VP, S, S', VP, S, S, S'\}$$
   $$path(3) = \{S, S', VP, S, S\}$$

   b. $[_{S'}$ who$_2$ $[_S$ everyone$_3$ $[_S$ do you think $[_{S'}[_S$ e_2 saw e_3 at the rally]]]]]

   $$path(2) = \{S, S', VP, S, S, S'\}$$
   $$path(3) = \{VP, S, S', VP, S, S\}$$

These structures exhibit the same contrast in path structure as the parallel single clause sentences. That is, only when the quantified phrase is the subject do we derive a structure that can be interpreted as representing an ambiguity. Where the quantifier is the object, such a structure gives rise to an ill-formed path structure. Instead, the quantifier must be adjoined to some node within the complement clause, a position from which its path will not intersect with that of the *wh*-phrase. But in such a structure it can only be interpreted as having narrower scope.

Note that eschewing the ECP does away with one of the problems mentioned above. Since the addition of the complementizer *that* to (12a) will not affect the relevant path structure, *Who do you think that everyone saw at the rally* will be predicted to be as ambiguous as its complementizer-less counterpart. (I will return later to those contexts in which we do find *that*-trace effects.)

So far these results are just the ones we have argued to follow from the ECP, except that no reference need now be made to linear adjacency. Moreover, the PCC can be extended in a uniform way to account for superiority effects, avoiding the government-adjacency asymmetry for the ECP discussed above. Continuing with our assumption that multiple interrogation constructions, at LF, involve adjunction to NP in COMP, the relevant structures are (14) and (15); as discussed in chapter 3, in such structures we can identify the "head" of COMP as the (unique) phrase that is immediately dominated by COMP:

(14) *Who admires what?*

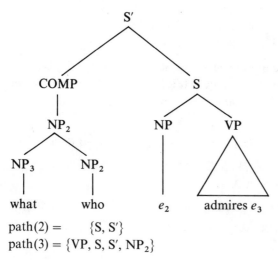

path(2) =   {S, S'}
path(3) = {VP, S, S', NP_2}

(15) *What does who admire?

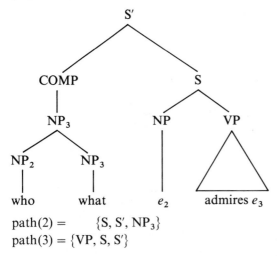

path(2) =   {S, S', NP$_3$}
path(3) = {VP, S, S'}

In these structures the effect of adjunction to NP is (so to speak) to extend the categorial path; this makes a difference in (15), since to "reach" the binding phrase, path(2), originating in the subject position, must now cross an NP$_3$ node, that is, the node to which it is adjoined. But then the paths illicitly overlap, violating the PCC. This contrasts with (14), in which the paths properly embed. Bear in mind that in evaluating path structure it has been presumed that the higher occurrence of the NP to which the LF-moved phrase has been adjoined—NP$_2$ in (14) and NP$_3$ in (15)—is sufficient to terminate a path.[7]

As noted in Chiba (1977) and Kayne (1983), "superiority" violations in sentences like *What did who admire are considerably ameliorated when another wh-phrase is added; hence the improved grammaticality of ?What did who admire when. Following essentially the ideas of Kayne (also adopted in Pesetsky (1982)), we can account for this by assuming that the PCC is evaluated, with respect to a given COMP at LF, with respect to the union of all the nonhead wh-paths to that COMP. For the basic superiority case just considered this will be of no consequence, since there is only one nonhead path. But when we consider What did who admire when, we must consider the union of the paths of who and when. Supposing that when is an underlying daughter of VP and is attached to NP$_3$ at LF,[8] then the relevant structure will be (16):

(16) ?*What did who admire when?*

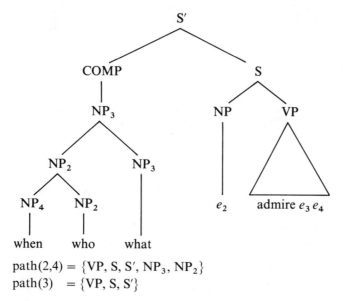

path(2,4) = {VP, S, S', NP$_3$, NP$_2$}
path(3)   = {VP, S, S'}

In contrast to (15), then, this structure will be consistent with the PCC.

Returning now to multiple interrogation structures that contain just a pair of *wh*-phrases, notice that a minimal contrast parallel to the one just observed is also found with *why*-questions (and similarly *how*-questions). Thus, we find ?*Why did Harry buy what* opposed to the ungrammatical **Why was what bought by Harry*. Though such cases may be amenable to analysis via the ECP under certain extensions of that condition,[9] under the PCC they will be analyzed exactly like the cases just discussed. To see this, however, we must elaborate the assumptions we have made so far about the basic phrase-structure configuration of English, namely, that the INFL(ection) node is immediately dominated by S. Pesetsky (1982) has argued in considerable detail, however, that INFL is immediately dominated by a further intermediate projection, INFL', reminiscent of the PredP node of Chomsky (1965), which we will take as a nonmaximal level in the S'-projection. This elaboration will have no effect at all on the analysis of the cases above, but will have consequences for the analysis of *why*-questions, presuming that *why* is an adverbial daughter of INFL'. Then the relevant structures will be (17) and (18):[10]

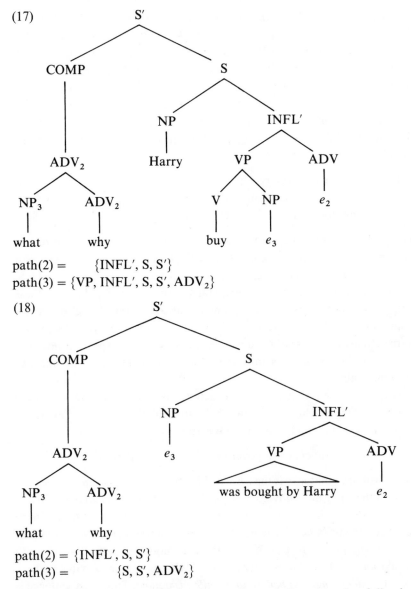

(17)

path(2) =   {INFL', S, S'}
path(3) = {VP, INFL', S, S', ADV$_2$}

(18)

path(2) = {INFL', S, S'}
path(3) =   {S, S', ADV$_2$}

The analysis of these sentences extends to ruling out the following examples, with *why* understood as a complement modifier:

(19)a. *Why does who believe that John came?
    b. *Why does John believe (that) who left?

In each case the path of *why* is {INFL', S, S', VP, INFL', S, S'}, which illicitly overlaps with the path of *who* at LF; in (19a) this is {S, S', ADV}, and in (19b) it is {S, S', VP, INFL', S, S', ADV}. Note that (19b) is ill-formed regardless of whether *that* is present or not. This further indicates the irrelevance of the ECP.

Before we continue, another comment is in order regarding multiple *why*-questions—namely, why must *why* be moved to COMP in S-Structure? All of the following questions, in which this does not happen, are ill-formed:

(20)a. *Who believes Harry why?
   b. *Who believes that John came why?
   c. *Who does Harry believe left why?

The problem is that the paths associated with the LF-representations of these sentences are in fact consistent with the PCC. Taking the simplest structure as an example, note that the LF-path of *why* in (20a), {INFL', S, S', NP}, contains the path of *who*, which is simply {S, S'}. Each of these sentences, however, is quite ungrammatical. And even though there are examples like *Who does Harry believe why* that do violate the PCC, if this were actually the cause of the deviance, then we would expect the addition of another *wh*-phrase, as in *Who does who believe why*, to improve grammaticality.

It appears, then, that some other factor is at work, independent of path structure. One possibility is that the source of the deviance lies in the following general condition on modification:

(21) At LF, modifiers must govern the constituent they modify.

Now assuming that *why* is the *wh*-word for S-modifying *because*-clauses, it follows that they must govern S at LF. Where *why* is the head of COMP—that is, when it has been moved at S-Structure—this condition will be satisfied directly, since S' will be the minimal maximal projection dominating the *why*-phrase in COMP and the S it modifies. Note that *why* will always *modify* the S that is sister to its COMP; this is true even in sentences like *Why does Angleton believe that Philby is a mole*. Thus, this sentence is an inquiry into the causation of a belief, be it direct (into the cause of the belief itself) or indirect (into the cause of the action that gave rise to the belief). This distinction corresponds to whether *why* was an underlying constituent of the matrix (direct) or complement (indirect) clause; but in either case it is the entire sentence that is modified by *why*.

The required structural relation for modification, however, will not be found in the LF-representations of the sentences in (20). This is because *why* will be adjoined to NP in COMP, and the boundary of this NP will block government outside of its projection. This is shown schematically in (22):

(22)

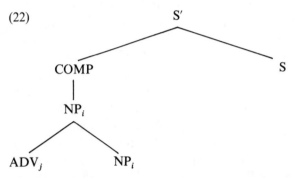

Structures with a COMP of this form will violate (21), since the adverbial modifier will not govern the constituent it modifies. Notice that a *because*-clause at LF, which we take to be a daughter of INFL' at this level, will satisfy the condition, since the minimal maximal projection dominating it is S', INFL' being nonmaximal. Since this is also the sole maximal projection dominating S, S will be governed consistently with (21).[11]

The correctness of this analysis is further confirmed by the contrast between (20a) and (23), which expresses the same meaning as the former example would, if it were grammatical:[12]

(23) Who believes Harry for what reason?

The difference here is that it is not the entire modifying phrase that is moved at LF, as in (20a), but rather only the *wh*-phrase, which is a constituent of the modifier. Thus, in (24) the government requirement on modification is satisfied, since the prepositional phrase, now containing a trace of movement, still governs the clause it modifies:

(24) $[_{S'}[\text{what reason}_3 [\text{who}_2]] [_S e_2 [_{\text{INFL}'} \text{believes Harry } [_{\text{PP}} \text{for } e_3]]]]$

As the reader can verify, this structure will be associated with a consistent path structure. Also, note that this account argues that prepositions may be stranded in LF-representations; but consider the contrast of (23) with (25):

(25) *What reason does who believe Harry for?

But this sentence is associated with an ill-formed path structure; the path of *who*, which is {S, S', NP}, since it is adjoined by LF-movement to the phrase already residing in COMP, overlaps with the path {PP, INFL', S, S'} of *what reason.*[13]

If we follow the suggestion of chapter 3 that multiple quantification structures do not involve adjunctions to S, as depicted in (7) and (8), but instead involve adjunction to NP, then the analysis will proceed just as described for the superiority cases. The only difference is that rather than occurring in COMP, the clustering of quantified phrases will be adjoined to S; the relations of the paths, however, will remain the same. On the other hand, presuming that the COMP position is reserved for *wh*-phrases, the mixed quantifier-*wh* structures will continue to involve one phrase in COMP, the other adjoined to S. But even with this difference, the uniformity of treatment provided by the PCC accords with the intuition that the subject-object asymmetries observed in the multiple interrogation and mixed quantifier-*wh* constructions—one arising as a distinction in grammaticality, the other as a difference in range of interpretation—are part and parcel of a single phenomenon.

Pursuing this line of analysis, recall the problem with an ECP account of superiority—namely, that there are apparent superiority effects that do not seem to fall under the ECP. (3) was one example; others are illustrated in (26) through (28):

(26)a. I wondered who to persuade to read what books.
  b. *I wondered what books to persuade who to read.

(27)a. Who does Mary expect to buy what?
  b. *What does Mary expect who to buy?

(28)a. Who did you tell about what topic?
  b. *What topic did you tell who about?

In each case, in the LF-representations of both the (a) and the (b) examples, both traces of the *wh*-phrases will be in lexically governed, and hence properly governed, positions. Thus, it would seem that the ECP could not distinguish these cases. However, the PCC can, again on the assumption that movement to COMP in LF involves adjunction to NP in COMP. To take an example, consider the LF-representation of (27a) and (27b), exceptional Case-marking constructions:

(29)

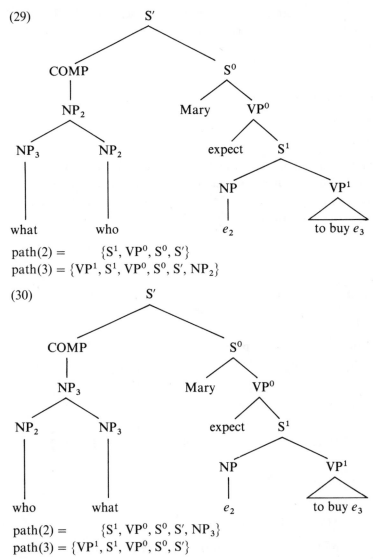

path(2) = $\{S^1, VP^0, S^0, S'\}$
path(3) = $\{VP^1, S^1, VP^0, S^0, S', NP_2\}$

(30)

path(2) = $\{S^1, VP^0, S^0, S', NP_3\}$
path(3) = $\{VP^1, S^1, VP^0, S^0, S'\}$

Given the PCC, these cases are distinguished as desired. In (29) the categorial path from e_2 to the phrase that binds it is properly embedded in the path from e_3 to its binder, a circumstance that fails to obtain in (30). In the latter structure the paths overlap rather than embed, and thus this structure is ill-formed. Exactly the same path structures are to be found in (26a–b) and (28a–b), as the reader can verify.

Interestingly, the PCC can also account for the curious fact that although preposition stranding is permissible in a sentence like *Whom did John buy a book for*, it is proscribed in its multiple interrogation counterpart (31):

(31) *Whom did John buy what for?

(31) further contrasts with (32a–b), which are on a par grammatically:

(32)a. For whom did John buy what?
    b. What did John buy for whom?

Here again we cannot invoke the ECP; as with the structurally comparable sentences in (28) (for which parallel facts can be adduced), all the empty categories at LF will be properly governed. But now consider the path structure, taking the structure at LF of (31) first:

(33)

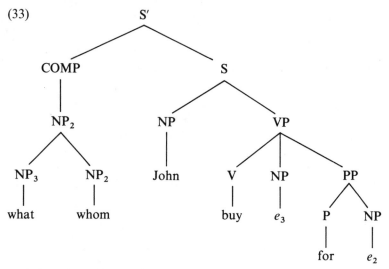

path(2) = {PP, VP, S, S'}
path(3) =   {VP, S, S', NP$_2$}

In the relation of path(2) and path(3) we see the now familiar outlawed pattern of path overlap. However, in the LF-representations of (32a) and (32b) we instead find the lawful embedding of paths; this is because in each structure both path(2) and path(3) commence at the same node.

(34)

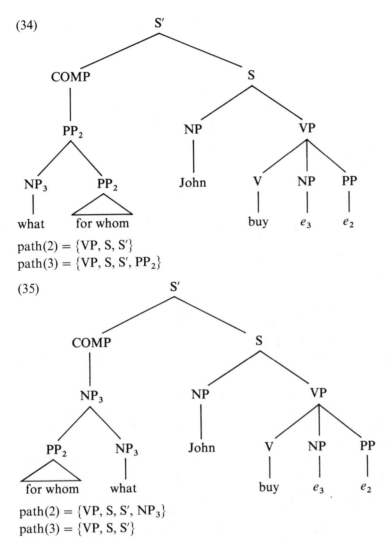

path(2) = {VP, S, S′}
path(3) = {VP, S, S′, PP₂}

(35)

path(2) = {VP, S, S′, NP₃}
path(3) = {VP, S, S′}

Thus, assuming that the PCC is the applicable constraint on LF-representations, we can further account for the asymmetries found in pre-position stranding in singular and multiple interrogation constructions.[14]

One other case worth mentioning is (36), discussed in chapter 3, due to Van Riemsdijk and Williams (1981):

(36) Who knows which pictures of whom Bill bought?

This example can be construed as a multiple direct question with respect to the pair *who* and *whom*.[15] This construal will be represented as follows:

(37) $[_{S'}[_{NP}$ whom$_3$ [who]] $[_S e_2$ knows $[_{S'}$[which pictures of $e_3]_4$ $[_S$ Bill bought $e_4]]]]$

$$
\begin{array}{lll}
\text{path}(2) = & & \{S, S'\} \\
\text{path}(3) = \{PP, N', NP_4, & S', VP, INFL', & S, S', NP_2\} \\
\text{path}(4) = & \{VP, INFL', S, S'\} &
\end{array}
$$

Here path(2) and path(3) intersect, and the former properly embeds in the latter. Path(4), on the other hand, intersects with neither of the other paths: it has no members in common with path(2), and with path(3) it has no common path segment, since the two share only a single member node. So this structure too is well-formed at LF.[16]

Movement from VP-Adjoined Position

Given the considerations of the previous section, let us now suppose that whatever the status of the ECP, it is not a condition on LF-representation. Instead I shall assume the PCC, which refers to the relation of binding paths in a structure, as the relevant constraint. Taking this view, however, apparently raises its own problems, for there are cases in which the ECP was invoked that cannot be reduced to the sort of interactive effects that fall under the PCC. In particular, recall the contrast between the presentational *How many spies did there walk into the room from Russia and the existential *How many spies were there from Russia*. This was attributed to failure of proper government of the VP-adjoined position in the former, but in the latter, in which the trace of the moved *wh*-phrase is the subject of a small clause complement, proper government obtained. But if we do not assume the ECP to be relevant, then there is no contrast to be drawn along this dimension to distinguish these examples. How can we account for their differential grammaticality, if neither the ECP nor the PCC is relevant?

Let us first consider the analysis of presentational *there*-sentences in more detail.[17] They will have the S-Structure in (38):

(38) $[_{S'}[_S$ there$_2$ $[_{VP}[_{VP}$ walked into the room] many spies$_2]]]$

As discussed in chapter 3, the postposed VP-adjoined NP will be in a "subject" position for θ-role assignment, since it is governed by VP. Note that we have assumed that *there* and *many spies* are coindexed, following the assumption that the latter phrase has been postposed from the D-Structure [NP, S] position. (In fact, we need not even assume that the formative *there* is even present at S-Structure; we may instead consider it to be the spell-out of an empty expletive category occurring in a given structural position (see Chomsky (1981, 85–89)). However, exactly how *there* is treated in this regard will not be relevant here.)

Subsequent *wh*-movement of the postposed phrase will result in the following structure for the ungrammatical *How many spies did there walk into the room*:

(39) [$_{S'}$ how many spies$_2$ [$_S$ there$_2$ [$_{VP}$[$_{VP}$ walk into the room] e_2]]]

The problem with this structure becomes apparent when we attempt to determine just what category serves as the variable bound by the *wh*-phrase. It cannot be *there*, since *there* is expletive and hence pronominal, and variables, by assumption, are nonpronominal. Consequently, it must be the trace of *wh*-movement; but this category is not locally $\bar{\text{A}}$-bound; its local binder is *there*, which occurs in an A-position. Thus, the *wh*-phrase binds no variable at all, and (39) can therefore be ruled out by appeal to the prohibition against vacuous operators. In accounting for its deviance no mention need be made of the ECP or proper government.

As under the previous analysis, LF-movement to S from the S-Structure representation in (38) will also be ruled out, since it too will give rise to a vacuous operator. But once again an LF-representation in which there has been adjunction to VP will be well-formed:

(40)

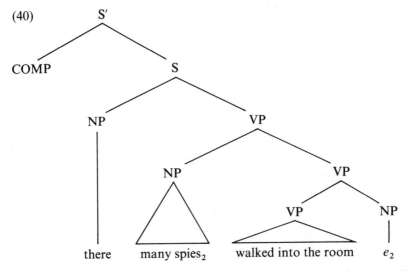

Here e_2 will not be locally A-bound by *there*, but rather will be locally $\bar{\text{A}}$-bound by *many spies*, so that in this case it will qualify as a variable. All other previous considerations regarding this structure will carry over, except that we no longer need concern ourselves with whether the empty category is properly governed or not.

We now turn to existential *there*-sentences. Since we are following Stowell (1978) in maintaining that such sentences do not involve movement, *many spies* in (41) will occur in the same position in D-Structure and S-Structure. This means that it will not be coindexed with *there*, since no movement is involved in its derivation:

(41) [$_S$ there were [$_S$ many spies from Russia]]

Its LF-representation is (42):

(42) [$_S$ many spies$_2$ [$_S$ there were [$_S$ e_2 from Russia]]]

Since *there* bears no index (or, if it has an index, it is distinct from that of the preposed phrase and its trace), the local binder of e_2 is an $\bar{A}$-binder, and thus this category legitimately qualifies as a variable. *Wh*-movement is also well-formed; compare *How many spies were there from Russia*, which will have the same structure as (42), except that there is movement to COMP.

Given our line of analysis that eschews the ECP, then, the absence of proper government of the VP-adjoined position is no bar to movement. Insofar as movement is constrained from this position, the cause will be found elsewhere. This would lead us to expect movement to be possible from this position in a language in which there were no interfering factors such as those found in English presentationals. Italian is a much-discussed case in point; as Rizzi (1982) initially argued, *wh*-movement from subject in sentences such as *Chi credi che verrà* 'Who do you believe (that) will come' involves a derivational step in which the subject is first postposed and then moved to COMP. In this regard Italian takes advantage of the independent possibility of free subject inversion in the derivation of *wh*-constructions, so as to avoid occasioning, according to Rizzi, an ECP violation. That inversion is involved is reinforced by evidence from Italian dialects, brought out by Brandi and Cordin (1981) and discussed in detail by Safir (1982). For instance, Trentino has a lexical subject clitic *el* that coocurrs with [NP, S] subjects but must be absent with postverbal subjects. Thus, (43a) and (43b) are grammatical, but not (43c):[18]

(43)a. El Mario el   magna.
         Mario   SCL eats
         'Mario is eating.'
    b.   Magna el Mario.
         eats   Mario

   c. *El magna el Mario.
      SCL eats Mario

Wh-movement of a subject patterns like the postverbal cases; it prohibits occurrence of the subject clitic:

(44)a. Chi ha magnà algeri?
      who has eaten yesterday
  b. *Chi el ha magnà algeri?
      who SCL has eaten yesterday

These examples, then, show an even stronger result; whereas Rizzi proposed that "long" *wh*-movement from embedded subjects must be from the postverbal position, the argument just sketched indicates that "short" *wh*-movement must also be from this position. But these facts make it doubtful that inversion is involved because of the ECP. Though long movement would be from an immediately postcomplementizer position, presumably short movement would be directly into COMP, and this should constitute proper government under the coindexing clause of the ECP.

    Why is *wh*-movement of subject required to be from the postverbal position in Italian—now taken as a legitimate position of movement—and what are the structural conditions that warrant it? Let us suppose, basically following ideas of Chomsky (1982), that in a "pro-drop language" like Italian, empty subject categories are always pronominal. Such pronominals bifurcate into referential, normally found in pro-drop structures like (45a), and expletive, found in free inversion structures like (45b). Such empty pronominal elements will be designated by *pro*:

(45)a. *pro* mangia.
        eats
     '(He) eats.'
  b. *pro* mangia Gianni.
         eats   Gianni.
     'Gianni eats.'

The exact status of each type of *pro* will depend on its exact relation to AGR(eement) and the θ-Criterion; thus, in (45a) *pro* is referential and bears a θ-role, but in (45b) the θ-role is assigned to the postverbal NP, and *pro* is expletive. See Chomsky (1982) and Jaeggli (1984) for discussion of how these assumptions are to be specifically incorporated into the grammar.

    Assuming now that all empty subjects occurring at S-Structure in Italian are pronominal, it follows that they can never be variables; as mentioned above, variables are by definition nonpronominal categories. Thus, if there were direct *wh*-movement from subject position, the resulting structure would be ill-formed, again because there would be a quantifier that binds no variable at all. Thus, (46) is ruled out:

(46) $[_{S'}$ chi$_2$ $[_S$ credi $[_{S'}$ che $[_S$ *pro*$_2$ verrà]]]]

The problem here is that this structure has, so to speak, been mistakenly identified as involving pro-drop.

Since the empty category arising from direct movement (either short or long) from the [NP, S] subject position to COMP will be *pro* and hence cannot be a variable, it follows that *wh*-movement must be from some other position in which a variable can occur. This position is the postverbal position, so that (47) will be well-formed:

(47) $[_{S'}$ chi$_2$ $[_S$ credi $[_{S'}$ che $[_S$ *pro* verrà e_2]]]]

In this structure *pro* is the expletive *pro* of free inversion; the postverbal subject will be the variable bound by the *wh*-phrase, legitimately so (assuming that expletive *pro* is not coindexed with the postverbal empty category; see Safir (1982)). Exactly the same considerations will require *wh*-movement from the postverbal position under short *wh*-movement.

To summarize: In this section we have seen that the facts about movement from postverbal position in English and Italian do not require that the ECP play any role. Dropping this condition allows movement from this position to be free, up to independent constraints arising from the definition of categories. Where movement is not possible, it is because the structure in question does not contain any category definable as a variable; such structures, therefore, contain vacuous operators, a circumstance that our discussion of extraposition has already shown to be prohibited at LF.[19]

"*That*-Trace" Effects: What's Left of the ECP?

An initial motivation for the ECP as a constraint on LF was that "*that*-trace" effects are found at this level. But as pointed out in the beginning of this chapter, matters are somewhat more complicated, for there are apparently LF-movements from the directly postcomplementizer position. Thus, *who* and *so* can be extracted and adjoined to the matrix in our original examples (1) and (2), respectively, since the former is interpreted as a direct question, the latter with coreference between *her* and *Mary*:

(1) Dean believed that whó had erased the White House tapes.

(2) I told her that so many people attended last year's concert that I
made Mary nervous.

Moreover, insofar as transparency is assumed to be syntactically represented at LF by quantifying in, then the ECP cannot be playing a role, since
Dulles believes that some agent is a mole is just as susceptible to being
understood de re as its counterpart without *that*, or as in a sentence in
which the quantified phrase is a complement object. Be this as it may,
however, it is clear that under the current view, examples like (1) and (2) are
now unproblematic. Since they involve the movement of only a single
operator, they do not call the PCC into play; and the ECP is no longer
relevant to determining their well-formedness. Similarly with the trace of
lowering in *A hippogryph is likely to be apprehended*. Indeed, the PCC is
strictly irrelevant to it; since it has no antecedent, being expletive, it has no
path.

   However, we are now left with having to account for those cases in which
"*that*-trace" effects apparently do occur; but we will see that matters are not
so clear cut. Consider first multiple interrogation. Although examples (48a)
and (49a) are ungrammatical, they sharply contrast with (48b) and (49b),
both of which are significantly better, if not perfectly well-formed:

(48)a. *Who does Dulles believe that who suspected?
    b. ?Who believes that who suspected Philby?

(49)a. *Who did Dulles wonder whether who suspected?
    b. ?Who wondered whether who suspected Philby?

The (a) and (b) examples differ in whether *wh*-movement at S-Structure has
been from the same clause as the LF-movement; when it is not, the resulting
sentence is considerably better than when both the S-Structure movement
and LF-movement are extractions from the complement. Why should these
examples contrast as they do? From the perspective of the ECP there
should be no difference, since in both the (a) and the (b) examples a *wh*-
phrase follows a complementizer, and extraction from this position will
lead to a violation in any event.[20] And this, as we shall see, is because the
ECP makes reference to a structural property—whether there is proper
government—and not to a structural relation. But what seems to be critical
in the contrasts in (48) and (49) is, in fact, the relation of the binding paths
found at LF; in the (a) examples they overlap, whereas in the (b) examples
they embed, and it is just this distinction to which the PCC, and not the
ECP, is sensitive. Taking (48) as an example, the relevant structures, with

their associated paths, are these:

(50)a. $[_{S'}[_{NP}[_{NP}\text{ who}_3]\text{ who}_2]\ [_S\text{ Dulles }[_{VP}\text{ believe }[_{S'}\text{ that }[_S\ e_3$
   $[_{VP}\text{ suspected }e_2]]]]]]$

   path(2) = {VP, S, S', VP, S, S'}
   path(3) =   {S, S', VP, S, S', NP$_2$}

   b. $[_{S'}[_{NP}[_{NP}\text{ who}_3]\text{ who}_2]\ [_S\ e_2\ [_{VP}\text{ believes }[_{S'}\text{ that }[_S\ e_3\text{ suspected}$
   Philby]]]]]

   path(2) =   {S, S'}
   path(3) = {S, S', VP, S, S', NP$_2$}

Interestingly, the contrast in question apparently does not disappear where deletion of the complementizer is possible; thus, although *Who does Dulles believe who suspected* is perhaps marginally better than (49a), it remains markedly worse that *Who believes who suspected Philby*. This is as expected, if the distinction turns on the relation of binding paths, as we are claiming. This is because path structure will not be altered by eliminating the complementizer in these examples.

It is with respect to the complementizer that there emerges a fundamental difference between "*that*-trace" effects at LF and the well-known contrast between *Who does Dulles believe suspected Philby* and **Who does Dulles believe that suspected Philby*, for in the latter contrast, presence vs. absence of the complementizer makes all the difference in grammaticality. The latter examples also differ from the LF "*that*-trace" cases in another way; whereas the LF examples clearly involve two movements to $\bar{A}$-positions, and hence two paths, the standard S-Structure "*that*-trace" violation involves a single movement to an $\bar{A}$-position, and thus apparently contains only a single path. In analyzing these cases, Pesetsky (1982) argues that this is, in fact, only apparent. On his proposal an S-Structure representation containing an extraction from an embedded clause will project a path from INFL to COMP, consisting of the nodes INFL', S, and S'. Thus, **Who does Dulles believe that suspected Philby* will be associated with the following path structure:

(51) $[_{S'}\text{ who}_2\ [_S\text{ does Dulles }[_{VP}\text{ believe }[_{S'}\text{ that }[_S\ e_2\ [_{INFL'}\text{ suspected}$
   Philby]]]]]]

   path(2) =   {S, S', VP, INFL', S, S'}
   INFL-COMP = {INFL', S, S'}

Here we find the illicit overlap of intersecting paths. If the complementizer is deleted, however, path(2) can be broken up into two parts, since now, the complementizer being absent, successive cyclic movement is possible. This will result in a structure in which there are no overlapping paths:[21]

(52) $[_{S'}$ who$_2$ $[_S$ does Dulles $[_{VP}$ believe $[_{S'}$ e_2 $[_S$ e_2 $[_{INFL'}$ suspected Philby]]]]]]

$$\text{path}(2) = \{S, S'\}$$
$$\text{path}(2') = \{S', VP, INFL', S, S'\}$$
$$\text{INFL-COMP} = \{INFL', S, S'\}$$

As Pesetsky argues in detail, assuming that there is an INFL-COMP path has utility in accounting not only for "*that*-trace" effects, but also for a range of other phenomena.[22] In the current context, however, a certain issue remains. If this path is relevant to the PCC at LF, it would incorrectly predict that (48a), *Who does Dulles believe that who suspected*, and (48b), ?*Who believes that who suspected Philby*, should be equally ill-formed and that the former should be significantly improved by deletion of *that*. That is, how are the differences between the LF "*that*-trace" cases and the S-Structure cases to be accommodated? The most straightforward way would be to assume simply that only at S-Structure, and not at LF, does the PCC take into account paths from INFL to COMP. In this regard LF will be distinguished from S-Structure, in part, not by the conditions that hold of each level, but rather in terms of the distinct structural properties of each relevant to general conditions. In fact, we can maintain that the PCC holds of all levels of syntactic structure—D-Structure, S-Structure, and LF— although at D-Structure its effect will be vacuous, since by definition at this level there is no Ā-binding.[23] In a sense, the notion that the INFL-COMP path "counts" only at S-Structure can be taken as a way of expressing that properties of the complementizer are relevant to well-formedness at S-Structure, but not at LF. At LF, insofar as we find "*that*-trace" effects, they are solely a function of the improper interaction of paths of movement and are not related to the complementizer. This makes a certain amount of sense, given that the central properties represented at LF pertain to binding, argument structure, and their interrelations. Complementizer deletion, where it is possible, does not affect what proposition is expressed by a complement clause, and by extension, we might assume, complementizer structure also does not interact with determining the well-formedness of binding at the level that represents the structurally determined semantically relevant properties of sentences.

Returning now to the main thread of our discussion, "*that*-trace" effects at LF, recall the contrast between the examples in (53), which were initially discussed in chapter 2:

(53)a. Who thinks everyone saw you at the rally?
   b. Who do you think everyone saw at the rally?

(53b) is ambiguous; (53a) is not. This is because only (53a) can be associated with an LF-representation that has a consistent path structure and in which the Scope Principle is satisfied. The relevant structures are as follows:

(54)a. $[_{S'}$ who$_2$ $[_S$ everyone$_3$ $[_S$ e_2 thinks $[_{S'}[_S$ e_3 saw you at the rally]]]]]

   path(2) =   {S, S, S'}
   path(3) = {S, S', VP, S, S}

   b. $[_{S'}$ who$_2$ $[_S$ everyone$_3$ $[_S$ you think $[_{S'}[_S$ e_3 saw e_2 you at the rally]]]]]

   path(2) = {VP, S, S', VP, S, S, S'}
   path(3) =   {S, S', VP, S, S}

Only (54b) is associated with a path structure in which the paths properly embed. Of course, (53a) can have an LF-representation in which the embedded quantifier is adjoined to some node lower than the matrix S. But then its path will not intersect with the path of the *wh*-phrase, and hence there will be no violation of the PCC. But in that case, the *wh*-phrase must be interpreted with broader scope.

   Note that the same judgments of interpretation hold if the complementizer *that* is present in (53). But this is as expected, since the presence or absence of the complementizer will not affect the paths relevant to well-formedness at LF. Of course, if the ECP were the relevant constraint, then we would expect (53b) to be as unambiguous as (53a), since extraction should be blocked from the position immediately following a lexical complementizer.

   Interestingly, a subject-object asymmetry is also found in the following pairs:

(55)a. Who remembers where Bill bought what?
   b. *Who remembers where who bought the piano?

(56)a. Who remembers why Bill bought what?
   b. *Who remembers why who bought the piano?

As is well known, the well-formed (a) examples are ambiguous between multiple direct and indirect questions. That the latter interpretation is excluded for the (b) examples is not surprising, since LF-movement to the complement COMP would simply be a "superiority" violation of the sort accounted for above; that is, it would reduce to the ungrammaticality of

Where did who buy the piano and *Why did who buy the piano*. What is perhaps surprising, on the other hand, is that the (b) examples are not grammatical as multiple direct questions; just as in (48b) and (49b), deriving their LF-representations involves movement to COMP from a different clause from that of the *wh*-phrase already residing in that position. Why should this be so?

The reason lies in the fact that the path of the phrase in the complement COMP equally well interferes with movement to the matrix; where these examples differ from those in (48) and (49) is that the latter examples contain complementizers, which do not generate binding paths, in the complement COMP. To see this, consider (57), the relevant LF-representation of (55b):

(57) $[_S[_{NP}[_{NP}$ who$_3]$ who$_2]$ $[_S$ e_2 $[_{VP}$ remembers $[_{S'}$ where$_4$ $[_S$ e_3 $[_{VP}$ bought the piano $e_4]]]]]]]$

$$\text{path}(2) = \qquad\qquad \{S, S'\}$$
$$\text{path}(3) = \qquad \{S, S', VP, S, S', NP_2\}$$
$$\text{path}(4) = \{VP, S, S'\}$$

The problem arises in the relation of path(3) and path(4); whereas path(2) embeds into path(3) (and has no interaction with path(4)), path(3) and path(4) overlap. This is sufficient to rule out (57) as a violation of the PCC. In the LF-representations associated with (55a), on the other hand, no such problem arises; both (58a) and (58b) have well-formed path structures:

(58)a. $[_{S'}$ who$_2$ $[_S$ e_2 $[_{VP}$ remembers $[_{S'}$ $[_{NP}[_{NP}$ what$_3]$ where$_4]$ $[_S$ Bill $[_{VP}$ bought e_3 $e_4]]]]]]$

$$\text{path}(2) = \qquad\qquad \{S, S'\}$$
$$\text{path}(3) = \{VP, S, S', NP_4\}$$
$$\text{path}(4) = \{VP, S, S'\}$$

b. $[_{S'}[_{NP}[_{NP}$ what$_3]$ who$_2]$ $[_S$ e_2 $[_{VP}$ remembers $[_{S'}$ where$_4$ $[_S$ Bill $[_{VP}$ bought e_3 $e_4]]]]]]$

$$\text{path}(2) = \qquad\qquad \{S, S'\}$$
$$\text{path}(3) = \{VP, S, S', VP, S, S', NP_2\}$$
$$\text{path}(4) = \{VP, S, S'\}$$

In each case where paths intersect, one embeds properly into the other, as required by the PCC. Notice that if there were a structure in which path(4) were extended—that is, in which movement were from a more deeply embedded position than the point of origin of path(3)—a violation of the PCC would arise. This is what we find in examples like *Who remembers where Bill told who that Harry bought a book.* This sentence is grammatical, but only with *where* interpreted with *tell*; excluded is a construal on which it is interpreted with *buy*. This is as expected, since the latter interpretation would give rise to the unwarranted path extension just described.

It seems, therefore, that the "*that*-trace" effects in multiple interrogation structures can be subsumed under the PCC. But what of the initial cases that motivated taking the ECP as a condition on LF, the contrast in French with the polarity item *personne* in (59), discussed in chapter 2?

(59)a. ?Je n'ai exigé qu'ils arrêtent personne.

b. *Je n'ai exigé que personne soit arrêté.

Kayne's (1981b) original idea was that *ne* functions as a "scope marker" in these examples, so that in a sense they too reflect an interaction between *personne* and *ne*. How is this to be characterized? Following ideas developed in Pesetsky (1982), suppose we assume that associated with *ne* is a path from the complement to the matrix INFL, so that the sentences in (59) will have the LF-representations and path structures indicated in (60):

(60)a. $[_S$ personne$_2$ $[_S$ je n'ai $[_{VP}$ exigé $[_{S'}$ que $[_S$ ils $[_{INFL'}$ $[_{VP}$ arrêtent $e_2]]]]]]]$

path(2) = {VP, INFL′, S, S′, VP, INFL′, S, S}
path(ne) =   {INFL′, S, S′, VP, INFL′}

b. $[_S$ personne$_2$ $[_S$ je n'ai $[_{VP}$ exigé $[_{S'}$ que $[_S$ e_2 $[_{INFL'}[_{VP}$ soit arrêté]]]]]]]$

path(2) =   {S, S′, VP, INFL′, S, S }
path(ne) = {INFL′, S, S′, VP, INFL′}

Assuming that *ne* also generates a path thus gives the desired contrast, without recourse to the ECP.

In each of the sentences under discussion *personne* occurs within a subjunctive complement. If we take the existence of a path from the lower to the higher INFL to be in part a function of this, then we can also account for the distinction in scope possibilities, also pointed out in Kayne (1981b), between *Angleton demanded that the CIA arrest nobody* and *Angleton demanded that nobody be arrested by the CIA*. Though the distinction is perhaps less robust than in French, note that only the former is compatible with Angleton having made no demands at all. Apparently, however, the subjunctive-indicative distinction is quite clear in Catalan, as discussed in Picallo (1984) with respect to a number of different phenomena that pattern similarly with respect to broad scope of quantification. Among them are negative quantifiers, which can take broad scope when in object position, but which can only have this type of interpretation when in subject position if contained in an indicative complement. The relevant examples are (61a) (indicative) and (61b) (subjunctive) (Picallo's (75), (76)), broad scope being prohibited only in the former:

(61)a. En Pere no creu que *ningú* no l'estima.
   'Peter does not believe that nobody neg loves him/her.'

   b. En Pere no creu que *ningú* no l'estimi.
   'Peter does not believe that nobody neg love him/her.'

The contrast can be directly accounted for on the assumption that there is an INFL-INFL path associated with the LF-representation of subjunctive, but not indicative, sentences in Catalan. Then LF-movement in indicatives will be free, since there is no other path to cause a conflict with the path arising from movement, but it will be limited to non-[NP, S] positions in subjunctives. In the latter structures circumstances will be as in French; paths of movement from object will properly include the INFL-INFL path, but not those of movement from preverbal subject.

The Italian polarity item *nessuno* 'nobody' behaves like French *personne*. As discussed in Rizzi (1982), *nessuno*-sentences display the same basic properties as *personne*-sentences; extraction is possible from object position, but not from subject:

(62)a. Non pretendo che tu   arresti nessuno.
   neg require   that you arrest nobody
   b. Non pretendo che nessuno ti   arresti.
   neg require   that nobody you arrest

We may assume that the analysis developed for the French examples can be carried over here, so that the impossibility of a broad scope construal in (62b) is a result of improper path structure at LF, where the paths of *nessuno* and *non* will intersect but not embed.

Another factor comes into play here, however, since Italian, unlike French, allows free subject inversion. Thus, according to Rizzi, broad scope over the matrix clause is possible for *nessuno* when it occurs as an inverted postverbal subject, adjoined to VP within the complement clause, but not for its nonpostposed counterpart (63b):

(63)a. Non pretendo che sia arrestato nessuno.
   neg require   that be arrested nobody
   b. Non pretendo che nessuno sia arrestato.
   neg require   that nobody be arrested

That this should be so is not surprising, given that *wh*-movement is also possible from this position; indeed, Rizzi's claim is that this case will be structurally isomorphic to the parallel *wh*-construction at LF, differing only in that in one case movement from the VP-adjoined position occurs in the mapping onto S-Structure, whereas in the other case it occurs in the mapping onto LF. Note that in the LF-representation of (63a) the path from the VP-adjoined position to the matrix S will overlap that of *non*.

Allowing that the derivation onto LF of *nessuno*-constructions at least in part mimics the derivation onto S-Structure of *wh*-constructions raises a question: Why can't the derivation of the LF-representations of *nessuno*-sentences *fully* mimic that of *wh*-constructions? That is, why can't there be a derivation for (63b) in which *nessuno* is first postposed and then extracted to the higher clause, with both movements occurring in the mapping onto LF? If this derivation were possible, then it would predict, incorrectly, that the sentence could have a broad scope construal; (63b) would, in fact, be no different than (63a). However, this derivation will be ruled out on the assumptions we have already developed. Recall that in Italian, empty [NP, S] categories are identified, at S-Structure, as pronominal. Lexical categories at this level, on the other hand, receive no such status, and moving them in the derivation onto LF will not give rise to *pro*. (Although in English, where there is no such identification, expletive categories may arise in mapping onto LF, as in the "lowering" structures discussed in chapter 4.) Thus, in (64), derived from the S-Structure of (63b), we must take the [NP, S] empty category as a variable, since it is $\bar{\text{A}}$-bound, and hence as an argument:

(64) nessuno$_2$ [$_S$ non pretendo [$_{S'}$ che [$_S$ e_2 [$_{VP}$[$_{NP}$ sia arrestato] e_2]]]]

But then what is the status of the VP-adjoined empty category? It cannot also be an argument, since it would then form a chain with the preverbal position; this would in turn violate the θ-Criterion, since there would be only one θ-role associated with the two arguments in the chain. The alternative is that it is an operator, a possibility because the VP-adjoined position can also be taken as an $\bar{\text{A}}$-position, as discussed in chapter 3. But what variable does it bind? Clearly not the [NP, S] category; that is bound by *nessuno*. It can only be taken as a vacuous operator, but this is prohibited. Thus, if there is inversion in mapping onto LF, it is not possible to extract via further LF-movement.[24] Notice that this does not prohibit LF-movement directly from the [NP, S] position; this is perfectly permissible so long as the resulting structure does not violate any other conditions, as would happen in (62), in which such movement would lead to a contravention of the PCC. Thus, nonnegative quantifiers, for instance, can be assigned broad scope by movement directly from this position.

Turning to polarity quantifiers in English, in particular *any*, note that its distribution is unconcerned with the presence or absence of the complementizer, as the equal grammaticality of *Philby doesn't believe that anyone suspects Burgess* and *Philby doesn't believe anyone suspects Burgess* attests. Given the assumption that *any* is a broad scope quantifier, this means that we do not want to postulate a path between the polarity quantifier and its negative trigger, as we did for French and Italian.[25] That there is no such path in English, however, is not to say that the distribution of *any* does not observe constraints otherwise associated with the outputs of LF-movement. For instance, the outputs of LF-movement are apparently subject to a "Specificity Constraint," which blocks $\bar{A}$-binding into certain domains. The effect of this condition can be seen in contrasting the ambiguity of *John's pictures of everyone are hanging on the wall* with the lack of ambiguity in *John's picture of everyone is hanging on the wall*; the latter example has only the narrow scope "relative"-type construal discussed in chapter 3. Presuming that singular (as opposed to plural) NPs are specific, this follows, since binding into such domains is proscribed. The effect of this proscription on *any* can be seen in the following contrast, from May (1977):

(65)a.   John never reads books which have any pages missing.
   b.   *John never read the book that has any pages missing.

In this regard the properties of *any* are apparently parallel to those of other quantifiers.[26]

To summarize: I have been arguing in this chapter that the Path Containment Condition should be taken as a condition on representations at LF, replacing the ECP. All of the effects attributed to the ECP in preceding chapters can be elegantly accounted for by the PCC. Thus, given this condition, the constraints on multiple quantification, quantifier-*wh*, and superiority sentences can be seen to be of a piece, a general and intuitively pleasing result. With regard to "*that*-trace" phenomena, the PCC gives the correct results for LF, where these effects are to be found only where there is a conflict between paths of movement to $\bar{A}$-position. S-Structure "*that*-trace" effects, which have somewhat different properties regarding presence of the complementizer, are the result of a path from INFL to COMP, whose relevance is peculiar to S-Structure. At LF, where there is but a single operator, no "*that*-trace" effects are observed, again supporting the overall view.

Paths and Pronouns: Crossover and Related Problems of Bound Variable Anaphora

To this point in the discussion of paths and path structure I have considered only those paths whose roots are empty categories. But do we want to restrict the domain of path theory in this way? In this section I will explore the ramifications of answering that we do not, that instead paths are more generally associated with *all* Ā-bound elements, regardless of whether they are lexical or not. More specifically, I will examine the consequences of assuming that locally Ā-bound pronouns generate paths to their binders, and thus that they may be interpreted as bound variables only in those representations that project well-formed path structures. As we shall see, assuming that pronominal paths are members of path structures allows us to directly account for some of the central issues of bound variable anaphora, including crossover, "reconstruction," and crossing coreference.

Perhaps the best place to start is with the most well-known constraint on bound variable anaphora: weak crossover. Thus, consider (66), the structure associated with *Who does his mother admire*:

(66)

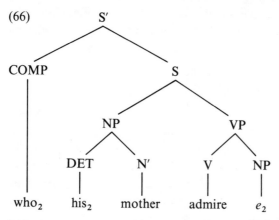

This structure contains two elements that are locally Ā-bound; thus, under our current assumptions it will be associated with two paths, one projected from the pronoun, the other from the trace. These paths are as follows:

path(his$_2$) = {NP,   S, S′}
path(e_2)   =   {VP, S, S′}

These path structures violate the PCC; they overlap on the nodes S and S′, but each contains a node not contained in the other. Thus, (66) is ill-formed, in contrast to the structure of *Who admires his mother*, given in (67):

(67)

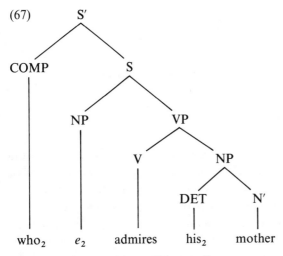

who₂   e₂   admires   his₂   mother

This structure contains only a single $\bar{\text{A}}$-path, that of the trace. The pronoun generates no path at all, since it is locally A-bound by the trace. Since there is just one path, there can be no conflict with the PCC. Similarly, there is no inconsistency in the structure associated with *His mother admires John* at LF; since this structure has no element in an $\bar{\text{A}}$-position, it is associated with no paths at all.

   Other cases of weak crossover can also be seen to follow if all $\bar{\text{A}}$-bound categories give rise to paths. Thus, consider the contrast, discussed in chapter 3, between *Every pilot hit some MIG that chased him* and *Every MIG that chased him hit some pilot*. Although the pronoun in the former sentence can be taken as a bound variable just when the *every*-phrase has broader scope, no bound variable interpretation is available in the latter, regardless of the scope relations of the quantifiers. Let us consider the former example first. As discussed above, it can be associated with two LF-representations, one in which both quantified phrases are attached to S, the other in which only the subject is attached to this projection, the object NP being attached to VP.[27] They differ in that in the latter the scope relations of the quantifiers are fixed, whereas in the former they may freely vary. The structures are given in (68):

(68)a. [$_S$[$_{NP}$ some MIG that chased him$_2$]$_3$ [$_S$[$_{NP}$ every pilot$_2$] [$_S$ e_2 hit e_3]]]

$$\text{path}(e_2) \quad = \quad \{S, S\}$$
$$\text{path}(\text{him}_2) = \{\ldots NP, S, S\}$$
$$\text{path}(e_3) \quad = \{VP, \quad S, S, S\}$$

b. [$_S$[$_{NP}$ every pilot$_2$] [$_S$ e_2 [$_{VP}$[$_{NP}$ some MIG that chased him$_2$]$_3$ [$_{VP}$ hit e_3]]]]

$$\text{path}(e_2) = \{S, S\}$$
$$\text{path}(e_3) = \quad \{VP, VP\}$$

(In (68a) and below the ellipses stand for the nodes traversed within the complex noun phrase.) If we take the pronoun as a bound variable in (68a), and therefore as coindexed with the *every*-phrase, then the structure runs afoul of the PCC. This is because the path of the pronoun and the path of the trace of the *some*-phrase overlap on two S nodes, but each contains other nodes not shared with the other. (68b), on the other hand, is well-formed. Here the pronoun is no longer Ā-bound; its local binder is the empty category in the subject position. That is, it is A-bound and therefore not associated with a path. The other two paths, those of the traces of LF-movement, do not overlap at all and thus do not fall within the purview of the PCC.

We can thus account directly for the correspondence of scope and bound variable anaphora where the pronoun is contained within the object. But what happens when it is contained in the subject, as in *Every MIG that chased him hit some pilot*, in which the pronoun cannot be interpreted as a bound variable? In contrast to the case just discussed, this sentence has only one LF-representation in which the pronoun is Ā-bound, one in which both quantified phrases are adjoined to S. (Adjunction of the subject to VP—which would constitute an illicit downgrading movement—would simply not bring the pronoun within the c-command domain of the object NP.) The structure under consideration, then, is (69):

(69) [$_S$[$_{NP}$ some pilot]$_3$ [$_S$[$_{NP}$ every MIG that chased him$_3$]$_2$ [$_S$ e_2 hit e_3]]]

$$\text{path}(e_2) \quad = \quad \{S, S\}$$
$$\text{path}(\text{him}_3) = \{\ldots NP, S, S\}$$
$$\text{path}(e_3) \quad = \{VP, \quad S, S, S\}$$

For all intents and purposes the path structure of (69) is the same as that of (68a), except that now the pronoun is bound by the object, rather than by the subject. And as before, this structure is ill-formed; hence the impossibility of any bound variable interpretation for the pronoun. Of course, if the pronoun bore an index distinct from that of either of the quantified phrases and hence could not be interpreted as a bound variable, the resulting structure would be well-formed, with the quantifiers construable as freely varying in scope, since they govern one another.

This analysis of crossover in multiply quantified sentences assumes that bound variable anaphora is possible in just the same structures as under the analyses of Koopman and Sportiche (1982) and Safir (1984). Though these differ in that Safir's proposal allows for multiple A-binding of type-identical phrases (i.e., either all traces or all pronouns), they will each equally well mark as ill-formed the LF-representations of weak crossover sentences. For Koopman and Sportiche this is because the A-binding is nonbijective, for Safir because it is asymmetric. These proposals are not without their problems, however, mainly because instances of bound variable anaphora do exist in just the proscribed type of environment. To see this, consider the sentences in (70), with their LF-representations in (71), which Koopman and Sportiche and Safir can account for correctly:

(70)a. It is despised by somebody from every city.
    b. Whose mother does he admire?

(71)a. [$_s$[every city$_2$ [somebody from e_2]]$_3$ [$_s$ it$_2$ is despised by e_3]]
    b. [$_{s'}$[who$_2$ [e_2's mother]]$_3$ [$_s$ he$_2$ admires e_3]]

Bound variable anaphora is not possible in (70a–b), since in each case an operator (asymmetrically) locally Ā-binds a trace and a pronoun; in (71a), for instance, this is by *every city*. An initial virtue of this account then is that it eliminates any need for some sort of structural "reconstruction" in the case of (70b).

The problem arises with the examples in (72), which do admit bound variable anaphora:

(72)a. Somebody from every city despises it.
    b. Whose mother admires him?

These examples will be represented at LF as follows:

(73)a. [$_s$[every city$_2$ [somebody from e_2]]$_3$ [$_s$ e_3 despises it$_2$]]
    b. [$_{s'}$[who$_2$ [e_2's mother]]$_3$ [$_s$ e_3 admires him$_2$]]

In these structures the operators, *every city* and *who*, respectively, locally c-command (and hence $\bar{\text{A}}$-bind) a trace and a pronoun, just as they do in (71). Consequently, by Safir's principle, bound variable anaphora should not be possible, contrary to fact.

A comparable difficulty arises in the analysis of crossing coreference sentences like *Every pilot who shot at it hit some MIG that chased him.* As we have seen, both pronouns in these sentences can be construed simultaneously as bound variables, on either scope ordering of the quantifiers. In order for the pronoun contained within the subject NP to be bound, it must be c-commanded by the object NP, which therefore must also be adjoined to S. But then the latter phrase will $\bar{\text{A}}$-bind the pronoun as well as its trace, which is purportedly the illicit environment, once again a counterfactual result.

These problems do not accrue solely to accounts stated in terms of $\bar{\text{A}}$-binding, as in Safir (1984) or Koopman and Sportiche (1982), but are endemic to other accounts of bound variable anaphora, whether stated in terms of leftness (Chomsky (1976), Higginbotham (1980)) or c-command (Reinhart (1983)). Thus, taking as an example the contrast between *Somebody from every city despises it* and *It is despised by somebody from every city*, the former analysis predicts that bound variable anaphora should be possible for both examples, since in their LF-representation the trace of QR that serves as the antecedent of the pronoun is to its right (compare (70a) and (73a)), whereas the latter predicts that bound variable anaphora should be excluded in both, since in neither case does the quantified expression (at S-Structure, or its trace, at LF) c-command the pronoun. These problems have not gone unnoticed; both Higginbotham (1980) and Safir (1984) have added stipulations to their theories to account for these sorts of observations. But rather than considering the relative merits or demerits of these particular proposals, I will instead consider further crossover cases and the other problems of bound variable anaphora within the context of the assumptions developed in this chapter.

Turning first to the inverse linking cases, consider the contrast between (70a) and (72b). Recall that the LF-representation of inverse linking involves adjunction of the S-Structure embedded quantified phrase to its containing NP. The resulting structures are shown in (74a–b), the former representing the structure of *It is despised by somebody from every city* and the latter that of *Somebody from every city despises it.*

(74)a.

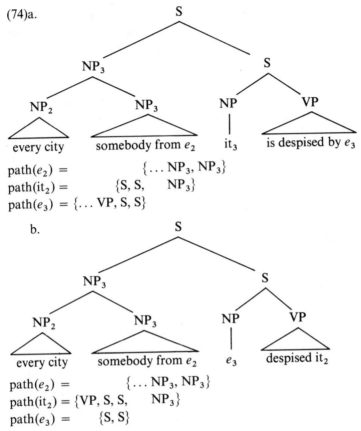

$$\text{path}(e_2) = \qquad \{\dots \text{NP}_3, \text{NP}_3\}$$
$$\text{path}(\text{it}_2) = \qquad \{\text{S, S}, \qquad \text{NP}_3\}$$
$$\text{path}(e_3) = \{\dots \text{VP, S, S}\}$$

b.

$$\text{path}(e_2) = \qquad \{\dots \text{NP}_3, \text{NP}_3\}$$
$$\text{path}(\text{it}_2) = \{\text{VP, S, S}, \qquad \text{NP}_3\}$$
$$\text{path}(e_3) = \qquad \{\text{S, S}\}$$

These two structures contrast in just the appropriate fashion with respect to their path structure. In (74a) there is a conflict between the path of the pronoun in subject position and the path rooted in the trace in object position. Although they overlap with respect to the S nodes, the former uniquely contains the NP node, and hence the path segment {S, NP}, whereas the latter contains the VP, and thus the segment {VP, S}. This violation of path consistency is not found, however, in (74b). In this case the path of the subject empty category properly embeds in that of the object pronoun, so there is no bar to taking the pronoun as a bound variable.

Interestingly, donkey-sentences exhibit the same sort of subject-object asymmetry as sentences involving inverse linking. Thus, no anaphoric interpretation is possible in *It is beaten by everyone who owns a donkey*, in comparison to *Everyone who owns a donkey beats it*; Higginbotham (1983b) makes the same observation, but with *wh* donkey-sentences. In chapter 3 I argued that at LF the representation of donkey-sentences involves adjunction to NP, just as with inverse linking, and that the pronoun is $\bar{A}$-bound at this level. Given this, it is no surprise to find just the same sort of crossover effects as with inverse linking, and the path structures of the LF-representations of the above sentences, found in (75), will be precisely the same as those in (74). The first structure is that of *It is despised by everyone who owns a donkey*; the second is that of *Everyone who owns a donkey beats it*:

(75)a.

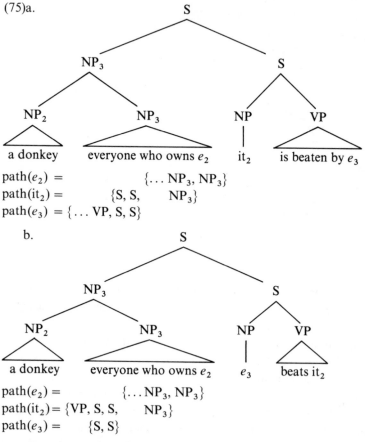

path(e_2) = $\{\ldots NP_3, NP_3\}$
path(it$_2$) = $\{S, S,$ $NP_3\}$
path(e_3) = $\{\ldots VP, S, S\}$

b.

path(e_2) = $\{\ldots NP_3, NP_3\}$
path(it$_2$) = $\{VP, S, S,$ $NP_3\}$
path(e_3) = $\{S, S\}$

Notice that in the NP-adjoined structure representing inverse linking sentences and donkey-sentences, the paths of the NP-adjoined phrases do not in any case intersect with the paths originating in either the subject or the object position (although they do share a member with the paths of the pronouns). Rather, the well-formedness of these structures depends solely on the relations of the paths originating from the subject and object, only the configuration in which the subject is empty and the object a pronoun being proper. The subject-object asymmetry of bound variable anaphora, then, reduces to a subject-object asymmetry in path structure.

Now consider the other sort of reconstruction case mentioned above, where a quantified phrase is embedded in a possessive NP—namely, (70b) and (72b), the contrast in anaphoric possibilities for the pronouns in *Whose mother does he admire* versus *Whose mother admires him*. The structures given above are repeated here, annotated with their path structures; recall our assumption that these structures also involve adjunction to NP:

(76)a. $[_{S'}[\text{who}_2 [e_2\text{'s mother}]]_3 [\text{he}_2 \text{ admires } e_3]]$
      $\text{path}(e_2) = \quad\quad \{NP_3, NP_3\}$
      $\text{path}(\text{he}_2) = \quad \{S, S', NP_3\}$
      $\text{path}(e_3) = \{VP, S, S'\}$
   b. $[_{S'}[\text{who}_2 [e_2\text{'s mother}]]_3 [e_3 \text{ admires } \text{him}_2]]$
      $\text{path}(e_2) = \quad\quad \{NP_3, NP_3\}$
      $\text{path}(\text{him}_2) = \{VP, S, S', NP_3\}$
      $\text{path}(e_3) = \quad\quad \{S, S'\}$

Once again these representations manifest the appropriate distinction in their path structures. In (76a) the only paths that overlap are those of he_2 and e_3; in (76b) these paths nest. And indeed only in the sentence corresponding to the latter is an anaphoric interpretation available.

As mentioned in chapter 3, the sort of cases discussed in the last few paragraphs have often been thought to require some sort of "reconstruction" in order to obtain an appropriate LF-representation. The idea was this: if it was supposed that *Whose mother does he admire* had an LF-representation like (77),

(77) $[\text{who}_2 [\text{he admires } [e_2\text{'s mother}]]]$

then the impossibility of anaphora would fall under the same restriction against a pronoun c-commanding its antecedent that accounts for the lack of an anaphoric connection in *He admires Oscar's mother*. Arguably this constraint is what accounts for very similar cases of "strong" crossover like *Who does he admire*. Now the analysis developed here of course obviates the need for any sort of reconstruction. But in doing so, it also implicitly denies the validity of the generalization from "strong crossover" to "reconstruction"—that is, that the lack of anaphora in *Who does he admire* and *Whose mother does he admire* is due to restrictions on binding from A-positions. Rather, the analysis embeds the claim that the appro-

priate generalization is between "weak crossover" and "reconstruction"—
that is, that there is a lack of anaphora in *Who does his mother admire* and
Whose mother does he admire because of restrictions on binding from
Ā-positions. In this regard I agree with the spirit, if not the letter, of both
Higginbotham (1980) and Safir (1984).

Let us turn now to crossing coreference sentences, where the problem is
to account for the possibility of simultaneous binding in *Every pilot who
shot at it hit some MIG that chased him*. Its structure, which I give only
schematically, is as follows:[28]

(78)

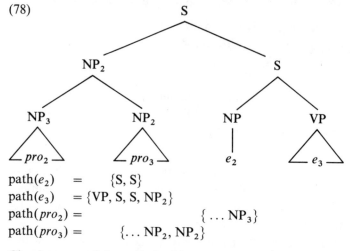

$$\text{path}(e_2) \quad = \quad \{S, S\}$$
$$\text{path}(e_3) \quad = \{VP, S, S, NP_2\}$$
$$\text{path}(pro_2) = \qquad\qquad\qquad \{\ldots NP_3\}$$
$$\text{path}(pro_3) = \qquad \{\ldots NP_2, NP_2\}$$

Clearly, none of the paths in this structure overlap; in fact, the only ones
that intersect—namely, those of the traces—properly embed. Neither of
the pronominal paths intersects with any other paths. Thus, here the
simultaneous anaphoric interpretation of the pronouns is perfectly permissible, representing the characteristic crossed binding pattern of these
sentences.

Assuming that all Ā-bound categories, be they empty or lexical, generate
paths thus permits a straightforward explanation of the central properties
of bound variable anaphora, without recourse to any special principles or
constraints. Rather, the observations regarding crossover, "reconstruction," and crossing simply follow from the general theory of Ā-binding.
However, one sort of problem remains to be considered. Many languages
allow the use of resumptive pronouns as a device for Ā-binding into
positions in which such binding of empty categories is proscribed. This is
even so in English in examples such as (79a), which sharply contrasts with

its counterpart in (79b), in which the pronoun is absent:

(79)a. ?John's the guy who I don't know whether he will be here or not.
  b. *John's the guy who I don't know whether will be here or not.

If pronouns project paths, we might expect both of these sentences to be ill-formed; thus, just as the path from the empty category in (79b) will conflict with the path from INFL to COMP, so should that of the pronoun in (79a). But we are assuming that the INFL-COMP path is only at S-Structure; suppose, following Chomsky (1982), that resumptive pronouns are only coindexed with their antecedents at LF. This would give the proper distinction, since at S-Structure the pronoun would be associated with no path, and at LF there would be no INFL-COMP path.

The approach just sketched predicts that since resumptive pronouns generate paths at LF, they should exhibit crossover effects. But this does not seem to be the case:

(80) Every student about whom Mary was wondering whether or not his professor failed him is sitting over there.

Why should this be so? The answer, I believe, lies in adapting the underlying idea of Safir's (1984) approach to path theory by incorporating the following condition on path structures:

(81) Union all coindexed type-identical paths.

That is, all paths originating in the same type of category (all empty categories or all pronouns) and bearing occurrences of the same index are unioned into a single path. Other paths that may be coindexed, but are projected from different category types, will count independently, as before. Examples like (80) now follow. Since both paths originate with pronouns, they will be unioned into a single path and as such cannot conflict with the PCC, in contrast to the paths in (82), which is a crossover violation:

(82) Every student about whom Mary was wondering who his professor failed is sitting over there.

The contrast in crossover is also found in other languages in which the use of resumptive pronouns is less marked than in English. Thus, in the following examples (from Hebrew and Irish, respectively), the pronoun cannot be construed as a bound variable in the (a) cases, in which there has been movement; but it can in the (b) cases, in which a resumptive pronoun is employed:[29]

(83)a. Miriám raatá et haíš se   imó   ahavá *e*.
        Miriam saw   man that mother-his loved

   b. Miriám raatá et haíš se   imó   ahavá otó
        Miriam saw   man that mother-his loved him
        'Miriam saw the man that his mother loved *e*/him.'

(84)a. Cén   fear a   sábháil a mháithair *e*?
        which man that saved   his mother

   b. Cén   fear a   sábháil a mháithair e?
        which man that saved   his mother   him
        'Which man did his mother save *e*/him?'

Other cases of multiple $\bar{\text{A}}$-binding also properly fall under the revised
path theory. Examples include parasitic gaps (*Which books did you read e
without filing e*) and the "gate" exceptions to crossover brought out in
Higginbotham (1980) (*Who did* [*PRO seeing his father*] *please e*). (Note that
the latter example shows that PRO and trace are type-nondistinct as far as
path theory is concerned.) Another interesting case is across-the-board
extraction, as in sentences like *I don't know anybody who Mary admires and
John despises*, whose path structure is consistent, as opposed to **I don't
know anybody who Mary admires him and John despises*, whose path structure is not. This is because the latter's path structure contains two paths,
which conflict, since the pronoun's path contains nodes solely from the left-
hand conjunct, whereas the empty category's path contains nodes solely
from the right-hand conjunct. However, all of the path segments defined by
these nodes will be in a single path in the path structure of the former
sentence. In fact, Pesetsky (1982) has argued that across-the-board constructions otherwise involve a joining of paths. He argues that the across-
the-board parallelism effects can be accounted for by assuming that the
INFL-COMP paths of each of the conjuncts are merged into a single path.
This predicts that across-the-board extraction will be possible just in case
the (merged) path of the empty categories is either contained within, or
contains, the (merged) INFL-COMP path. To see this, consider the path
structures in (85):

(85)a. I don't know anybody [$_{S'}$ who [$_{S^0}$ [$_{S^1}$ Mary [$_{INFL'}$ [$_{VP^1}$ admires *e*]]] and
        [$_{S^2}$ John [$_{INFL'}$ [$_{VP^2}$ despises *e*]]]]]

$$\text{path}(e) = \{VP^1, INFL', S^1, VP^2, INFL', S^{2,} S^0, S'\}$$
$$INFL\text{-}COMP = \quad \{INFL', S^1, \qquad INFL', S^2, S^0, S'\}$$

b. *I don't know anybody [$_{S'}$ who [$_{S^0}$[$_{S^1}$ Mary [$_{INFL'}$[$_{VP^1}$ admires e]]] and
[$_{S^2}$ e [$_{INFL'}$[$_{VP^2}$ despises John]]]]]

path(e)   = {VP^1, INFL$'$, S^1,   S^2, S^0, S$'$}
INFL-COMP =   {INFL$'$, S^1, INFL$'$, S^2, S^0, S$'$}

As can be readily observed, only the (a) structure is well-formed, since the
INFL-COMP path embeds in the path of the empty categories. The (b)
structure, on the other hand, contains no nested paths, and it is thus ill-
formed.[30] Pesetsky's analysis of across-the-board phenomena, then, can be
seen as simply one case of the functioning of the constraint that type-
identical paths are merged; since the INFL-COMP paths are type-
identical, they must be joined to form one path.

The proposed constraint on paths bears a certain similarity to the
condition proposed above for multiple interrogation structures—namely,
that the paths to all nonhead *wh*-phrases in a given COMP are unioned. We
might take this as indicative, and hold that unioning of paths with respect
to some condition of (type) identity is the only sort of condition that can be
placed on the structure of paths. If so, we can formalize path theory in
terms of the following two axioms, where "p" and "q" are paths, "S" is a
path structure, and "C" is a condition of the sort just mentioned:

(I) $\forall p, q \in S \, (p \cap q \rightarrow (p \subset q \vee q \subset p))$

(II) $\forall p, q \in S \, ((C \, (p) \wedge C \, (q)) \rightarrow p \cup q)$

In this way path theory can be defined set-theoretically, except for the
mention of condition"C," which refers to the structure from which the
paths are projected.

Notes

Chapter 1

1. Chomsky-adjunction of a constituent β to a node α yields structures either of the form "$[_\alpha \beta [_\alpha \ldots]]$" (left Chomsky-adjunction) or of the form "$[_\alpha [_\alpha \ldots] \beta]$" (right Chomsky-adjunction). In what follows the difference between right and left adjunction will turn out to be immaterial, since they manifest identical hierarchical constituent structures, but I will adhere to the convention of representing QR as effecting a left adjunction.

2. α c-commands β iff the first branching node dominating α dominates β (and α does not dominate β). This definition is essentially the one originally proposed in Reinhart (1976). In chapter 2 this definition will be modified along lines suggested in Aoun and Sportiche (1983).

3. See Higginbotham and May (1981a) for a formal analysis of the semantics of questions, as well as the discussion in chapter 2.

4. Note that assuming trace theory to apply generally to movement operations rules out the possibility of deriving something like S-Structure from something like LF by "lowering" quantified phrases, since such movements would give rise to structures containing unbound traces. Thus, the approach here is materially distinct from that of Lakoff (1971), for example.

5. With the further requirement that such functions assign the same value to $X \subset D$ as to values of automorphisms of D, one-to-one mappings from X onto itself.

6. Restricted quantifiers, in the defined sense, can be shown to have a number of properties. For instance, as shown in Higginbotham and May (1981a), they respect only the size of sets, and not the identity of their membership. Also, because such quantifiers encode effectively the same semantic information as the generalized quantifiers of Barwise and Cooper (1981), the results obtained there will carry over. Also see van Benthem (1983b).

7. This generalization apparently holds in other languages as well; for instance, it also characterizes the class of S-Structure preposable phrases in Hungarian, as discussed in Kiss (1981).

8. This example was brought to my attention by a reviewer.

9. Actually, the derivation will result in two equivalence classes of structures.

10. Linear order has often been claimed to strongly affect preferential order of interpretation. I am doubtful of the overall importance of this factor, however. In part this is because linear order is easily conflated with topic-comment relations; in most languages the subject precedes the object and corresponds to the discourse topic. And since topics take prominence in discourse, it is not surprising that when they are quantified phrases, they will have preferentially broad scope. Also, examples that purport to show the importance of linear order seem to me less than convincing. For instance, it is often held that in sentences with universal and negative quantifiers, scope is a function of precedence; see Halvorsen (1983) for a discussion of this. Examples like *No student admires every professor* and *Every professor is admired by no student* are taken to support this contention. But the latter example is considerably less than well-formed, and the former is interpretively suppletive with *No student admires any professor*. And it is instead the latter observations, it seems to me, that are in need of explanation.

11. These cases were pointed out to me by J. Higginbotham. Such examples have a third interpretation, on which no one is either loved or a lover. This is the independent interpretation; see the discussion in chapter 4. Note that this interpretation is also logically independent of either of the dependent interpretations; thus, for those who find one or the other of the latter construals difficult to obtain, the argument in the text will still go through, substituting the independent interpretation.

12. A semantically based filter would also be inappropriate here. If the grammar generates a class of representations each expressing, under an interpretation, correct truth-conditions, it would be otiose to filter some just to reconstruct them elsewhere in the system.

13. Cooper (1983) proposes that there are "quantifier meanings"—formally families of sets—and that quantifiers denote functions which characterize such sets as arguments of predicates. This gives the interpretation of multiply quantified sentences in which scope order mirrors surface order. For the inverse scope order a special mechanism is postulated that "stores," and later replaces, quantifier meanings. To a large extent this just recapitulates the functioning of QR, although without being subject to the grammatical constraints holding of QR and its output; see May (forthcoming).

14. For exposition I have ignored traces of cyclic movement in the embedded COMPs of the direct questions.

15. I have left aside the relation of this condition to the application of *wh*-movement in other constructions such as relative clauses and clefts.

16. We can capture this difference by maintaining that for English, but not Chinese, clause (a) of the *Wh*-Criterion must also be satisfied at S-Structure. There are also languages, such as Polish and Czech, that require that clause (b) be satisfied at

S-Structure and consequently allow multiply filled COMPs at this level (Toman (1981)).

17. For instance, Bach and Partee (1980), Evans (1980), Higginbotham (1980), Lasnik (1976).

18. This is pointed out in Heim (1982). There is more here than meets the eye, however, for only a broad scope interpretation is possible for this sentence if the pronoun is taken nonanaphorically, or if a proper name is substituted, as in *Every man admires the woman John loves*.

19. Note that it is not precluded that types of phrases may cross-classify, as has been argued for indefinite phrases. See Fodor and Sag (1982) for discussion.

20. Care is needed in clarifying just what is meant by "nonreferential," for it must be taken to denote a type of phrase and not whether tokens in fact make reference to actual objects. Thus, *Pegasus* does not refer in the latter sense, but it is a referential phrase.

21. Thanks are due to P. Ludlow for discussion of this point.

Chapter 2

1. Although Ladusaw assumes the analysis of May (1977), his basic ideas on the relation of LF to its interpretation carry over to the current framework.

2. That the grammar assigns sentences of this type only one logical form is also a central tenet of the analysis of Kempson and Cormack (1981). They propose that representing multiple quantification involves postulating just one logical form that expresses the logically weakest of a sentence's interpretations, regardless of the logical relation that may hold among the various construals. Any other interpretations are to be arrived at by conditions semantically strengthening the single logical form provided by the grammar. These procedures either "generalize," replacing existential by universal quantifiers, or "uniformize," reversing the scope order universal-existential to existential-universal. Thus, associated with *Everybody loves someone* will be a logical form with the universal-existential scope order, the stronger existential-universal order arising via the uniformizing procedure. For Kempson and Cormack multiple quantification represents a special case, the more general circumstance for their analysis being found with multiple numerical sentences, which they analyze as containing covert existential and universal quantifiers. In this case uniformizing and generalizing derive representations of the various interpretations—themselves not necessarily logically related—from a single form that itself does not fully express any complete construal of the sentence, but is rather "neutral" among them; see chapter 4 for some discussion of numericals. But even without delving into the exact details of Kempson and Cormack's proposal, we can see a number of problems that accrue to it. For instance, it is unclear just why the grammatically given logical representation should express a definite interpretation for multiple quantification sentences, but not for multiple numerical sentences, or

just what procedures are to be invoked to obtain an initial semantic representation from a sentence's syntactic structure. Moreover, the analysis runs into difficulty with sentences like *Nobody loves nobody*. If this is to be analyzed along the same lines as other multiple quantification sentences, then its single logical form should express one of its interpretations. But which one? With sentences of mixed universal and existential quantification, the universal-existential interpretation is logically weaker; but since the interpretations of *Nobody loves nobody* are logically independent, neither is weaker. Even more seriously, regardless of which representation is taken as basic, application of the uniformizing and generalizing procedures, as Kempson and Cormack state them, will not give rise to the other interpretation, taking the negative quantifier as a negated existential. Thus, taking the representation in which the object has broader scope, the "everyone is loved" interpretation is represented, but all the others that can be derived are not, in fact, interpretations of *Nobody loves nobody*. There is no road to the "everyone is a lover" interpretation. Just the opposite circumstance obtains if the latter construal is taken as basic. Of course, one might assume a logical structure for such sentences beyond what I have imagined—perhaps, as with multiple numerals, a "weak" structure not itself representing any actual interpretation, but from which they can be derived by the procedures. But then, it would seem, the relation between syntactic and semantic structure would become rather arbitrary.

3. Examples of this sort are noted and discussed in Åqvist (1975), Groenendijk and Stokhof (1982), Hirschbühler (1978), Hull (1974), Karttunen (1977), Karttunen and Peters (1980), Keenan and Hull (1973), and May (1977).

4. The problematic status of these cases for this sort of view of scope determination is pointed out in May (1977, ch. 2, fns. 8 and 9).

5. Although, as H. Lasnik has pointed out to me, *Who did you buy everything for* seems to disfavor a broad scope construal for the quantified phrase.

6. This is of particular importance in considering (18b), for if the object NP is focused by placing stress on the determiner, this phrase will have broad scope, giving an interpretation parallel to that of *For each of Dickens's books, which of you has read it*. In fact, this will be so for all of the cases we have discussed; insofar as the object NP is focused, it will be construed with broader scope than the *wh*-phrase in COMP. Maximally broad scope is, however, the general property of focused NPs, which, I will argue in chapter 3, is accounted for on the assumption that they are adjoined to S'. From this position they will have scope broader than COMP, and it is this position from which they will not disturb proper government of the subject position. Thus, in constructing relevant examples it is important to control for this factor, as in the examples cited in the text.

7. Although I am maintaining that (19a–b) have distinct ranges of meaning, Karttunen and Peters deny this; see below in the text for discussion.

8. Although notice that if *those* is eliminated from the former example, then the *wh*-phrase apparently can only have broad scope.

9. This is a problem that afflicts proposals to represent scope ambiguities by some

form of indexing mechanism, such as those in Van Riemsdijk and Williams (1981) and Haïk (1984).

10. Certain issues of the precise formulation of the ECP arise at this point. For instance, Lasnik and Saito (1984) state the ECP in such a fashion that once it comes to be satisfied for a given empty category, it remains so at all subsequent derivational levels. Thus, if the ECP is satisfied at S-Structure, then nothing in the derivation to LF could change this. But this is precisely what happens in the derivation of (18), which is consistent with the ECP at S-Structure but not at LF. Under Lasnik and Saito's formulation, then, this structure would be well-formed, and we would expect to find ambiguities where we do not. I will consider the appropriate well-formedness conditions on LF-representations further in chapter 5.

11. Van Riemsdijk and Williams (1981) claim that anaphora is possible only when the *wh*-phrase in (25a) has scope broader than *every poet*, but when *each* is substituted for *every*, an anaphoric construal of the pronoun is possible only if the *wh*-phrase has *narrower scope*. Although this is not inconsistent with the view espoused in the text, I am doubtful whether it is correct; for me, *his* in (25a) can be bound by the *every*-phrase only if the latter has broad scope. Van Riemsdijk and Williams's argument is based on the claim that (25a) allows only what they call a "generic" answer, such as *His sonnets, his epic verse, and his love poems*, but not a "pair list" answer, such as *Yeats read "Leda and the Swan," Eliot, "The Waste Land," and Thomas, "Do not go gently into that good night."* Though I disagree with the latter judgment, note that whatever the source of the "generic" answer, it cannot simply be a matter of scope, since questions like *Which of the Bodleian's books are up for auction* can be answered *Their antiquarian volumes and first editions.* In this case neither scope nor anaphoric binding is at issue. What seems to be conflated with matters of scope here is that *wh*-questions can usually be freely answered by specifications either of types (generic) or tokens (pair list).

12. Note that the quantified NP could equally well be attached to the embedded S consistently with the ECP. This would represent an interpretation in which the phrase *each of Heller's books* has scope narrower than the matrix predicate, in contrast to (33), in which its scope is broader. But see chapter 3 for further discussion.

13. Things are less clear with restrictive relatives. Though *Every student who some professor admires will graduate* allows the expected ambiguity, it does not seem that *Every student who admires some professor will graduate* excludes a broad scope construal for the object quantified phrase in the way that (38b) does, although this construal is considerably more marginal. This may be because indefinites in relative clauses may have a secondary interpretation as a kind of quasi-referring expression. See Fodor and Sag (1982) for discussion.

14. This is somewhat inaccurate. *Wh*-phrases in fact apply to "proto-questions," which themselves are of category Q and which are derived by application of the "?"-operator to sentences of category S. But our simplification will be harmless in the present context.

Chapter 3

1. That QR applies in this fashion is also suggested in DeCarrico (1983).

2. This example is essentially the one found in Sag (1976); Williams (1977) presents slightly different sentences arguing to the same point.

3. It should be noted that the argument just outlined is not without its problems. Hirschbühler (1982) points to examples such as *A Canadian flag is hanging in front of every window, and an American flag is too*, in which it seems that *every window* can be understood as having broader scope over the subject phrase in both conjuncts. This observation seems incompatible with Sag's and Williams's examples; if, for instance, it was held that QR could apply after VP-reconstruction, which would account for Hirschbühler's examples, it is unclear what would block a parallel derivation for the example in the text, predicting a parallel ambiguity. This remains, then, an open issue.

4. I am indebted to O. Jaeggli for bringing this argument to my attention.

5. Williams (1983) seeks to employ these scope facts to argue against small clauses as constituents; briefly, he argues that if such constructions do not contain a complement clause, then there is no possibility for narrow scope interpretation. But given the present analysis, this argument is considerably weakened. Also see Safir (1983) for arguments against Williams's position.

6. Movement from the VP-adjoined position is possible in Italian, however, as discussed in Rizzi (1982). See the discussion in chapter 5.

7. Although for some reason the sloppy construal is less favored with a nonaction verb, as in *Nobody from New York adores its subways, but everybody from Tokyo does*. Though interesting, this is not relevant to the validity of Reinhart's diagnostic, which holds just in case sloppy identity is possible in a given structural configuration.

8. Further application of QR to the subject NP would derive an LF-representation for (30a) parallel to (30b).

9. Note that (31) violates Safir's parallelism constraint, employed above in the account of weak crossover. I return to this in chapter 5.

10. See Reinhart (1983), Haïk (1984). Reinhart (1983, chs. 5, 7) claims that examples like (26) do not admit of a bound variable construal (although she agrees that the quantifiers are inversely linked). I disagree with her judgments here, however; the examples she cites, given as (i)–(iii), all seem to me to quite easily allow bound variable anaphora:

(i) People from each of the small western cities hate it.
(ii) Gossip about every businessman harmed his career.
(iii) The neighbors of each of the pianists hate him.

11. Here I differ from Fiengo and Higginbotham (1980), who hold that NP-internal movement is to N′, although there is some evidence that this node is also a possible adjunction site. Examples like *Every search for two redheaded men failed*, pointed

out by a reviewer and attributed to B. Partee, have an interpretation in which the numerical phrase has "property-level" scope; that is, the universal quantification is over a type of search, not over searches that are for some object(s). If this is represented by N'-adjunction, then the numerical phrase would have intermediate scope between *every* and *search*.

12. See Haïk (1984), Heim (1982), Kamp (1984), and Reinhart (1984), to mention just some of the more recent discussions.

13. Such pair quantifiers are not to be confused with binary quantifiers, which are also interpretively defined over the basic singulary quantifiers, but which are associated with distinct syntactic and semantic analyses. Whereas both pair and binary quantifiers are quantifiers of many variables, binary quantifiers are decomposable compounds, but pair quantifiers are not. Moreover, they can be shown to be in complementary distribution, binary quantifiers being available only when there has been no additional variable selection. See Higginbotham and May (1981b) for an argument supporting the inapplicability of binary quantifiers to donkey-sentences, which is just the context in which pair quantifiers apply.

14. Note that it will only be empty categories in this situation that can be so selected; pronouns, which would be bound variables if within the scope of a quantifier, will be assigned the deictic interpretation otherwise assigned free pronouns.

15. My treatment of the phenomena discussed in this paragraph differs from that of Haïk (1984). The generalization she gives is that a donkey-pronoun must be within the S-Structure c-command domain of the NP containing its antecedent, and this is embedded in an analysis that encodes scope at S-Structure through an extension of indexing. Haïk refers to pronouns that are bound by elements that do not c-command them at S-Structure as "indirectly bound," to be distinguished from those that are c-commanded by their binders and hence are "directly bound." Although I agree with Haïk that donkey-pronouns are a distinct species of bound pronoun, being bound by a derived pair quantifier, I believe that her approach suffers from a number of serious defects. To cite one relevant in the current context, notice that donkey-pronouns have certain properties that distinguish them from true bound variable pronouns. For instance, with an *every*-phrase as an antecedent, a donkey-pronoun must be plural, whereas a bound variable must be singular; hence the contrast between *The owner of every car sold them* and *The owner of every car sold it*. (I will treat this difference in the text below.) Now, since Haïk maintains that "direct pronouns" are those whose binders c-command them at S-Structure, this means, as Haïk notes, that the first pronoun in a crossing coreference sentence like *Some pilot who shot at it hit every MIG that chased him* must be an indirect pronoun. But if it is, then we expect it to parallel other indirect pronouns, in particular, donkey-pronouns. But this is incorrect, since this first pronoun is bound by an *every*-phrase and is singular. The point about crossing coreference sentences is that *both* pronouns are interpreted as bound variables; to use the current nomenclature, both are directly bound. But this is exactly what follows if the possibilities of bound pronoun anaphora are determined at LF. Crossed binding sentences will have LF-representations in which each pronoun is within the c-command domain of its binder, and they will undergo interpretation via binary

quantification. (Note that a pair interpretation is excluded, as in the simple multiply quantified sentences discussed above.) On the other hand, the properties found in donkey-sentences will also follow, since they must be interpreted by pair quantifications, and the various constraints on this construction will follow from the syntax and semantics of such quantifiers, as outlined in the text.

16. As with inverse linking, it is dubious that these are instances of "donkey-sentences," as suggested by Bach and Partee (1980), since they require plural pronouns with *every*-phrases.

17. Or an additional level of representation, as Van Riemsdijk and Williams (1981) suggest. They propose that there is a intermediate level between D-Structure and S-Structure that is prior to *wh*-movement, and at which the binding constraints are to be stated. The validity of the suggested constraints would, of course, undermine the motivation for such a level from the examples currently under consideration.

18. Note that we could still hold that Subjacency accounts for island constraints with *wh*-movement, since, by hypothesis, this rule is permitted to move solely to the COMP position.

19. The observations in this paragraph were brought to my attention by K. Safir.

20. The analysis given here with respect to the ECP and indexing for superiority is very similar in spirit to that suggested in Aoun, Hornstein, and Sportiche (1981). The two differ in that Aoun, Hornstein, and Sportiche's analysis requires assuming a special rule to attain the proper structure of the indices, whereas on my analysis this simply follows from the properties of adjunction rules.

21. Note that I do not take "Absorption," as it is employed by Aoun, Hornstein, and Sportiche (1981) and Van Riemsdijk and Williams (1981), as constitutive of multiple *wh*-constructions. In fact, the use of Absorption in those papers departs from its initial use in Higginbotham and May (1981a), described in chapter 1. In that paper Absorption was taken to apply *optionally*, and its role was in characterizing the presuppositions associated with multiple singular *wh*-questions. Thus, *Which man admires which woman* allows answers consisting of a single one-to-one pair—the "singular" interpretation—or a set of such pairs—the bijective interpretation. On the semantics developed in Higginbotham and May (1981a) the former interpretation arises if the *wh*-phrases are taken as a pair of unary operators, so that Absorption has not applied, and the latter if those phrases are absorbed so as to form a single binary operator. Thus, although Absorption plays a key role in the interpretation of *wh*-questions, as they are represented at LF, it is not necessary for the well-formedness of such structures at this level.

Chapter 4

1. This is also pointed out in van Benthem (1983a).

2. Kempson and Cormack (1981) point out that there are actually two types of circumstances consistent with the interpretation just described. They distinguish between a "complete group" interpretation, on which the directors made five

movies in collaboration, and an "incomplete group" interpretation, which is consistent, for instance, with two directors individually making two movies each, and one director individually making one movie. In this case it remains true that there are just three directors and five movies. Schein (1984) also distinguishes these construals, referring to them as the *product* and *sum* interpretations. Schein points out, however, that although under either interpretation the quantifiers are scopally independent, only the former is accounted for under the standard semantics for branching quantifiers. One way to surmount this problem would be modify the semantics so that the distinction at hand would be no more than a vagueness, alternative ways of satifying the truth-conditions specified by the (independent) logical representation. I will not, however, pursue this here. For alternative analyses, see the references cited.

3. For ease of exposition I have assumed that each complex noun phrase is attached to S; all the considerations to follow will remain the same if there is successive adjunction to NP, in line with the adjunction constraint discussed in chapter 3.

4. For some this type of interpretation is more clearly found when the sort of nonstandard quantifier that most readily allows branching is substituted, as in *Most relatives of each villager and most relatives of each townsman hate each other*, pointed out by Barwise (1979). Also, note that although I have focused on inverse linking of the quantifiers along the "branches," they may also be understood with relative interpretations. This would be represented by having adjunction within NP, rather than to NP, as in (13).

5. In characterizing the trace of "lowering" in this way, I am drawing largely on ideas developed in Aoun (1982) and Safir (1982).

6. There is some disagreement in the literature whether multiple raising constructions in fact have multiple opaque interpretations. Thomason (1976) and Halvorsen (1983) maintain that they do, a judgment with which I concur, but this is denied by Aoun (1982), who argues that they have only a single narrow scope interpretation. If the latter view is correct, we could account for it, following Aoun, by requiring that expletives be not only governed, but also Case-marked. Aoun seeks to link his claim about these cases to the ungrammaticality of sentences like *There appears to seem to be a man in the garden*, but the status of these examples is unclear, given the improved status of ??*There appears to be believed to be a man in the garden* or the even better *There is certain to be believed to be a man in the garden*.

7. The question remains whether this category retains its status as PRO. Although this will be of no consequence here, since this structure will be ill-formed for other reasons, it is important for sentences such as *To discover gold is everyone's dream*, due to Higginbotham (1980), in which the PRO subject of the infinitive will be Ā-bound at LF by a quantified phrase. See Safir (1984) for a discussion of the importance of this for the contextual definition of categories.

8. Notice that an ambiguity parallel to that which we have been discussing for raising constructions is found in *A hippogryph may be apprehended*, on the epistemic construal of the modal. This can be explained if the subject is raised from a small clause complement to the modal, along lines suggested for existentials by Stowell

(1978). This ambiguity is not found when *may* is assigned the root construal. Perhaps this is because this is a case of control, the overt subject controlling a PRO subject of the small clause complement. My thanks to D. Sportiche and T. Stowell for discussion of this point.

9. In the following discussion I will gloss over a number of details that need to be argued for; for supporting argumentation, see Guéron and May (1984).

10. The (possible) cyclic movement of the head NP has been ignored here, since it will be immaterial in the account that follows.

11. Suppose that any element occurring in an $\bar{\text{A}}$-position at LF is an operator, so long as it is not also specified at D-Structure to occur in that position. (The latter proviso is needed to rule out taking the trace of *why* in *Why did you leave e* as an operator. Though it occurs in an $\bar{\text{A}}$-position, this position is also specified at D-Structure.) Then the cyclic trace of extraposition will qualify as an operator and will fall under the condition against vacuity.

Chapter 5

1. (2) is from Guéron and May (1984). There it is argued that the ECP does hold of LF, but (following Safir (1982)) that it does not apply to nonthematic categories, such as the trace of QP found in the LF-representation of result clauses.

2. Examples of this type, cited in Hendrick and Rochemont (1982), are attributed to P. Culicover.

3. I differ here somewhat from Pesetsky (1982), who limits path members to maximal projection categories.

4. Pesetsky also addresses himself to superiority effects in multiple interrogation, although in a less than satisfactory fashion, needing to employ artifices such as paths of infinite extent. As we shall see, no such unnaturalness attaches to the analysis developed here, which incorporates Pesetsky's constraint in the context of our assumptions regarding the constituency of LF-representations.

5. Adjunction cannot be to the phrase in COMP, since this would violate the *Wh*-Criterion, which only permits *wh*-phrases to be contained in a [+WH] COMP.

6. Note that COMP is not a member of the paths of the *wh*-phrases, since it is a specifier, not a categorial, node. Though this will be inconsequential for what follows, D. Pesetsky has pointed out to me that if COMP were included, ?*That's a book which I don't know where you bought* would be predicted to be as ill-formed as **That's a book which I don't know where was bought*. This is because, with COMP included, the paths associated with the first sentence, which will be {VP, S, S', COMP} for *where* and {VP, S, S', VP, S, S', COMP} for *which*, will not embed, improperly, just as will the paths of the second sentence, which are {VP, S, S', COMP} for *where* and {S, S', VP, S, S', COMP} for *which*. However, if COMP is deleted from these sets, then the paths of the first sentence will embed, but not the paths of the second, thus making the appropriate distinction in grammatical status for these sentences.

7. This account shows that it is *nodes* that are relevant to the definition of paths. If it were projections, then path(2) would embed in path(3), since NP_2 is not dominated by the NP_3 projection.

8. Although it will, in fact, be irrelevant whether it is attached to NP_2 and *who* is then attached to it.

9. See Huang (1982b), Lasnik and Saito (1984).

10. I remain neutral on the exact category assigned to *why*, using simply the portmanteau label "ADV." Nothing in what follows will turn on this, however.

11. Other elements, which are seemingly of the same notional category as *why*, do not appear to fall under the proposed modification principle. In particular, *when* can appear in non-COMP position, as in *Who ate when*, and can save superiority violations such as *Who ate what when*, which *why* cannot do: **What did who eat why*. Why there should be this asymmetry between syntactic and notional classes is unclear.

12. This was brought to my attention by Y. Takubo.

13. When the preposition is not stranded, grammaticality is much improved: *For what reason does who believe Harry*. This could be accounted for if, contrary to our assumptions in the text, *for what reason* were a daughter of S, rather than of INFL'. This would leave the results in the text unchanged, but would render the paths associated with the latter sentence, {S, S', PP} for *who* and {S, S'} for *for what reason*, consistent with the PCC, which would not be the case if INFL' were a member of the latter path. Also, notice that stranding is not possible in **What reason does John believe Harry for*. This will also follow if the PP is adjoined to S, for then the path of the *wh*-phrase will overlap with the S-Structure path from INFL to COMP; see the discussion below.

14. In the analysis of example (32b) I have assumed that LF-movement may pied pipe a preposition, whereas in the analysis of (23) I assumed that this need not be so. In fact, we can simply hold that this is a free option of LF-movement; in either case just one of the options will lead to a well-formed LF-representation. Note that if we eschew reconstruction, then we must allow that the semantic rules, however formulated, can take account of PPs in COMP.

15. That the *which*-phrase, here the head of the embedded COMP, cannot be so interpreted follows from the fact that moving it requires moving the *wh*-phrase embedded under it as well, and then it will not be possible to satisfy subcategorization properties, since the embedded [+WH] COMP will contain no *wh*-phrase.

16. (37) contrasts with **Whom do you know which picture of e Bill bought*; the deviance of this example, however, can be attributed to Subjacency, since S-Structure *wh*-movement cannot avail itself of the sort of cyclic movement that obviates the effect of this condition for LF-movements.

17. The analysis to follow was suggested to me by O. Jaeggli and is similar to the analysis in Pollock (1982).

18. Proper nouns in Trentino take determiners, so that the *el* of *el Mario* is not to be confused with the subject clitic (SCL).

19. If one wanted to maintain that postverbal empty categories did have to be properly governed, a possible line of analysis would be as follows. Let us suppose, following ideas developed extensively in Safir (1982), that Italian structures containing null subjects, including those in which the subject has been inverted, contain a lexically null subject clitic, which Safir takes to be a set of features of V. Thus, the structure of subject inverted clauses will be schematically as follows:

(i) $[_S \, e \, [_{VP}[_{VP} \, cl + V] \, NP]]$

In considering the thematic structure of such constructions, Safir posits the notion of "θ-set," which roughly is a class of positions that jointly qualify as a single θ-position. In Safir's terminology, the θ-set would collectively constitute a unique position on a θ-chain. In (i) the null subject clitic along with the adjoined NP and [NP,S] positions, which are governed by VP, form the "external θ-set" of V. Given this notion, let us further suppose, now going beyond Safir's presentation, that any bound element within a θ-set is properly governed only if some member of that θ-set is properly governed. If the clitic in (i) is properly governed, then, by extension, so are the other members of its θ-set, including the postverbal NP position. We might assume proper government to be established in this case by virtue of the relation of V, a proper governor, to the clitic. Alternatively, we might take it that the clitic + V unit is itself properly governed, by INFL(ection). Evidence for the latter view arises from examples like (ii):

(ii) Angleton suggested that Dulles eliminate moles in the CIA, and eliminate moles he did $[_{VP} \, e]$.

In VP-fronting constructions presumably the empty VP must be properly governed. Suppose the governor to be INFL, which will then properly govern VP, but not the subject, which it does not thematically select. But if VP is properly governed, then so is its head, which in structures like (i) contains the clitic, which is a member of the θ-set. Thus, on either view the trace arising from *wh*-movement from the postverbal position will be properly governed.

20. Lasnik and Saito (1984), who develop a rather elaborate ECP analysis, note the improved status of (48b) and propose that it is a "marked" case of proper government by INFL. But this counterfactually predicts that (48a) should be as well-formed as (48b).

21. Recall that since path(2′) shares only one member with path(2) and the INFL-COMP path, it does not intersect with either.

22. For instance, it affords an account of the asymmetry of extraction from NP— the so-called Subject Condition, which proscribes extraction in *Who was a picture of stolen by Willie Sutton* but not in *Who did Willie Sutton steal a picture of*; only in the former will the path of *who* not properly contain the INFL-COMP path.

23. Even if phrases are base-generated in $\bar{\text{A}}$-positions, presumably they will not be connected to empty categories by coindexing until some later derived level of representation; see the discussion below.

24. This result can also be obtained if we follow the analysis of note 19, so long as the conditions requiring complementarity of a lexical subject and a null subject clitic refer to S-Structure properties. Then *wh*-constructions can contain subject clitics, but constructions with *nessuno* cannot; hence, only in the former can a θ-set be established that will allow proper government of the VP-adjoined position.

25. This may be simply because *any* does not move at all, as suggested in Aoun, Hornstein, and Sportiche (1981). See Linebarger (1980) for a contrasting view.

26. Chomsky (1981, 235ff.) points to examples such as *I wonder who heard the claim that John had seen what*, which he finds acceptable even though *what* is in a specific context. Though such examples seem acceptable, the other type of example Chomsky cites, *Who heard John's stories about what*, seems to me better than its singular counterpart, *Who heard John's story about what*, parallel to the contrast noted in the text.

27. I presume the former type of structure for ease of exposition, modulo the discussion of chapter 3. I leave it to the reader to determine that the same result will follow if there is adjunction of the object phrase to the subject NP that has been adjoined to S, and to work through more complex examples like *Some pilot gave every woman he liked some book she enjoyed*, with bound interpretations for the pronouns, which require the successive NP-adjunction structure.

28. It turns out that crossing coreference sentences require the NP-adjunction structure. If the NPs were each adjoined to S, the paths of the two pronouns would overlap, as would these paths and that of the object NP.

29. The former examples were brought to my attention by H. Borer; the latter examples are due to J. McCloskey.

30. Assuming that the across-the-board parallelisms are a function of the INFL-COMP path predicts that if there were an across-the-board resumptive pronoun structure, there should be no parallelism constraint. Reasonably natural examples are hard to come by, but examples like *Do you remember that guy who Marty was dating his sister and his brother was dating Jane*, adapted from Safir (1984), do not seem all that bad.

References

Akmajian, A. (1975). More evidence for an NP cycle. *Linguistic Inquiry* 6, 114–130.

Aoun, J. (1982). On the logical nature of the binding principles: Quantifier lowering, double raisings of "there" and the notion empty element. In J. Pustejovsky and P. Sells, eds., *Proceedings of NELS 12*. GLSA, University of Massachusetts, Amherst.

Aoun, J., N. Hornstein, and D. Sportiche (1981). Some aspects of wide scope quantification. *Journal of Linguistic Research* 1, 69–95.

Aoun, J., and D. Sportiche (1983). On the formal theory of government. *The Linguistic Review* 2, 211–236.

Åqvist, L. (1975). *A New Approach to the Logical Theory of Interrogatives*. TBL Verlag Gunter Narr, Tübingen.

Bach, E., and B. Partee (1980). Anaphora and semantic structure. In J. Kreiman and A. Ojeda, eds., *Papers from the Parasession on Pronouns and Anaphora*. Chicago Linguistic Society, The University of Chicago, Chicago, Ill.

Barwise, J. (1979). On branching quantifiers in English. *Journal of Philosophical Logic* 8, 47–80.

Barwise, J. (1981). Scenes and other situations. *Journal of Philosophy* 78, 369–397.

Barwise, J., and R. Cooper (1981). Generalized quantifiers and natural language. *Linguistics and Philosophy* 4, 159–219.

Belletti, A., and L. Rizzi (1982). On the syntax of *ne*: Some theoretical implications. *The Linguistic Review* 1, 117–155.

Benthem, J. van (1983a). "Five easy pieces. In A. G. B. ter Meulen, ed., *Studies in Modeltheoretic Semantics*. Foris Publications, Dordrecht.

Benthem, J. van (1983b). Determiners and logic. *Linguistics and Philosophy* 6, 447–478.

Borer, H. (1981). On the definition of variables. *Journal of Linguistic Research* 1, 17–40.

Brandi, L., and P. Cordin (1981). On clitics and inflection in some Italian dialects. Ms., Scuola Normale Superiore, Pisa.

Burzio, L. (1981). *Intransitive Verbs and Italian Auxiliaries*. Doctoral dissertation, MIT, Cambridge, Mass.

Chiba, S. (1977). On some aspects of multiple *wh* questions. *Studies in English Linguistics* 5, 295–303.

Chomsky, N. (1957). *Syntactic Structures*. Mouton, The Hague.

Chomsky, N. (1965). *Aspects of the Theory of Syntax*. MIT Press, Cambridge, Mass.

Chomsky, N. (1976). Conditions on rules of grammar. In *Essays on Form and Interpretation*. North-Holland, New York (1977).

Chomsky, N. (1977). On *wh*-movement. In P. Culicover, T. Wasow, and A. Akmajian, eds., *Formal Syntax*. Academic Press, New York.

Chomsky, N. (1980). On binding. *Linguistic Inquiry* 11, 1–46.

Chomsky, N. (1981). *Lectures on Government and Binding*. Foris Publications, Dordrecht.

Chomsky, N. (1982). *Some Concepts and Consequences of the Theory of Government and Binding*. MIT Press, Cambridge, Mass.

Cooper, R. (1983). *Quantification and Syntactic Theory*. D. Reidel, Dordrecht.

Culicover, P., and M. Rochemont (1983). Stress and focus in English. *Language* 59, 123–165.

DeCarrico, J. (1983). On quantifier raising. *Linguistic Inquiry* 14, 343–346.

Engdahl, E. (1980). *The Syntax and Semantics of Questions in Swedish*. Doctoral dissertation, University of Massachusetts, Amherst.

Evans, G. (1980). Pronouns. *Linguistic Inquiry* 11, 337–362.

Fiengo, R. (1977). On trace theory. *Linguistic Inquiry* 8, 35–61.

Fiengo, R., and J. Higginbotham (1980). Opacity in NP. *Linguistic Analysis* 7, 395–421.

Fodor, J. D., and I. Sag (1982). Referential and quantificational indefinities. *Linguistics and Philosophy* 5, 355–398.

Geach, P. (1962). *Reference and Generality*. Cornell University Press, Ithaca, N.Y.

Guéron, J., and R. May (1984). Extraposition and Logical Form. *Linguistic Inquiry* 15, 1–31.

Groenendijk, J., and M. Stokhof (1982). Semantic analysis of *wh*-complements. *Linguistics and Philosophy* 5, 173–233.

Haïk, I. (1984). Indirect binding. *Linguistic Inquiry* 15, 185–223.

Halvorsen, P.-K. (1983). Semantics for Lexical-Functional Grammar. *Linguistic Inquiry* 14, 567–615.

Heim, I. (1982). *The Semantics of Definite and Indefinite Noun Phrases*. Doctoral dissertation, University of Massachusetts, Amherst.

Hendrick, R., and M. Rochemont (1982). Complementation, multiple WH and echo questions. Ms., University of California, Irvine, and University of North Carolina, Chapel Hill.

Higginbotham, J. (1980). Pronouns and bound variables. *Linguistic Inquiry* 11, 679–708.

Higginbotham, J. (1983a). The logic of perceptual reports: An extensional alternative to situation semantics. *Journal of Philosophy* 80, 100–127.

Higginbotham, J. (1983b). Logical Form, binding, and nominals. *Linguistic Inquiry* 14, 395–420.

Higginbotham, J., and R. May (1981a). Questions, quantifiers and crossing. *The Linguistic Review* 1, 41–79.

Higginbotham, J., and R. May (1981b). Crossing, markedness, pragmatics. In A. Belletti, L. Brandi, and L. Rizzi, eds., *Theory of Markedness in Generative Grammar*. Scuola Normale Superiore, Pisa.

Hintikka, J. (1974). Quantifiers vs. quantification theory. *Linguistic Inquiry* 5, 154–177.

Hirschbühler, P. (1978). *The Syntax and Semantics of Wh-Constructions*. Doctoral dissertation, University of Massachusetts, Amherst.

Hirschbühler, P. (1982). VP-deletion and across-the-board quantifier scope. In J. Pustejovsky and P. Sells, eds., *Proceedings of NELS 12*. GLSA, University of Massachusetts, Amherst.

Huang, C.-T. J. (1982a). Move WH in a language without *wh*-movement. *The Linguistic Review* 1, 369–416.

Huang, C.-T. J. (1982b). *Logical Relations in Chinese and the Theory of Grammar*. Doctoral dissertation, MIT, Cambridge, Mass.

Hull, R. (1974). *A Logical Analysis of Questions and Answers*. Doctoral dissertation, University of Cambridge.

Jackendoff, R. (1972). *Semantic Interpretation in Generative Grammar*. MIT Press, Cambridge, Mass.

Jacobson, P. (1977). *The Syntax of Crossing Coreference Sentences*. Doctoral dissertation, University of California, Berkeley. (Distributed by Indiana University Linguistics Club, Bloomington.)

Jaeggli, O. (1980a). *On Some Phonologically-Null Elements in Syntax*. Doctoral dissertation, MIT, Cambridge, Mass.

Jaeggli, O. (1980b). Remarks on *to* contraction. *Linguistic Inquiry* 11, 239–245.

Jaeggli, O. (1984). Subject extraction and the null subject parameter. In C. Jones and P. Sells, eds., *Proceedings of NELS 14*, GLSA, University of Massachusetts, Amherst.

Kamp, H. (1984). A theory of truth and semantic representation. In J. Groenendijk, T. M. V. Janssen, and M. Stokhof, eds., *Truth, Interpretation and Information*. Foris Publications, Dordrecht.

Karttunen, L. (1977). Syntax and semantics of questions. *Linguistics and Philosophy* 1, 3–44.

Karttunen, L., and S. Peters (1980). Interrogative quantifiers. In C. Rohrer, ed., *Time, Tense and Quantifiers*. Niemeyer, Tübingen.

Kayne, R. (1981a). ECP extensions. *Linguistic Inquiry* 12, 93–133.

Kayne, R. (1981b). Two notes on the NIC. In A. Belletti, L. Brandi, and L. Rizzi, eds., *Theory of Markedness in Generative Grammar*. Scuola Normale Superiore, Pisa.

Kayne, R. (1983). Connectedness. *Linguistic Inquiry* 14, 223–249.

Keenan, E., and R. Hull (1973). The logical presuppositions of questions and answers. In J. S. Petofi and D. Franck, eds., *Presuppositions in Philosophy and Linguistics*. Athenaum, Frankfurt.

Kempson, R. (1983). Definite NPs and context-dependence: A unified theory of anaphora." Ms., School of Oriental and African Studies, University of London.

Kempson, R., and A. Cormack (1981). Ambiguity and quantification. *Linguistics and Philosophy* 4, 259–309.

Kiss, K. (1981). Structural relations in Hungarian, a "free" word order language. *Linguistic Inquiry* 12, 185–213.

Koopman, H., and D. Sportiche (1982). Variables and the bijection principle. *The Linguistic Review* 2, 139–161.

Ladusaw, W. (1981). On the notion *affective* in the analysis of negative-polarity items. *Journal of Linguistic Research* 1, 1–16.

Ladusaw, W. (1983). Logical Form and conditions on grammaticality. *Linguistics and Philosophy* 6, 373–392.

Lakoff, G. (1971). On Generative Semantics. In D. Steinberg and L. Jakobovits, eds., *Semantics*. Cambridge University Press, Cambridge.

Lasnik, H. (1976). Remarks on coreference. *Linguistic Analysis*, 2, 1–22.

Lasnik, H., and M. Saito (1984). On the nature of proper government. *Linguistic Inquiry* 15, 235–289.

Lewis, D. (1975). Adverbs of quantification. In E. Keenan, ed., *Formal Semantics of Natural Language*. Cambridge University Press, Cambridge.

Liberman, M. (1974). On conditioning the rule of Subject-Auxiliary Inversion. In

E. Kaisse and J. Hankamer, eds., *Papers from the Fifth Annual Meeting of the North Eastern Linguistics Society*. Harvard University, Cambridge, Mass.

Linebarger, M. (1980). *The Grammar of Negative Polarity.* Doctoral dissertation, MIT, Cambridge, Mass.

May, R. (1977). *The Grammar of Quantification*. Doctoral dissertation, MIT, Cambridge, Mass. (Distributed by the Indiana University Linguistics Club, Bloomington.)

May, R. (1981). Movement and binding. *Linguistic Inquiry* 12, 215–243.

May, R. (1983). Autonomy, case, and variables. *Linguistic Inquiry* 13, 162–168.

May, R. (forthcoming). Review of R. Cooper, *Quantification and Syntactic Theory*." To appear in *Language*.

Montague, R. (1974). The proper treatment of quantification in ordinary English. In R. Thomason, ed., *Formal Philosophy: Selected Papers of Richard Montague*. Yale University Press, New Haven, Conn.

Parsons, T. (1980). *Nonexistent Objects*. Yale University Press, New Haven, Conn.

Partee, B., and E. Bach (1984). Quantification, pronouns and VP anaphora. In J. Groenendijk, T. M. V. Janssen, and M. Stokhof, eds., *Truth, Interpretation and Information*. Foris Publications, Dordrecht.

Pesetsky, D. (1982). *Paths and Categories*. Doctoral dissertation, MIT, Cambridge, Mass.

Picallo, M. C. (1984). The Infl node and the null subject parameter. *Linguistic Inquiry* 15, 75–102.

Pollock, J.-Y. (1982). Accord, chaines impersonnelles et variables. *Linguisticae Investigationes* 7.1.

Postal, P. (1974). *On Raising*. MIT Press, Cambridge, Mass.

Quine, W. V. O. (1955). Quantifiers and propositional attitudes. Reprinted in W. V. O. Quine, *The Ways of Paradox*, Random House, New York, 1966.

Reinhart, T. (1976). *The Syntactic Domain of Anaphora*. Doctoral dissertation, MIT, Cambridge, Mass.

Reinhart, T. (1983). *Anaphora and Semantic Interpretation*. Croom Helm, London.

Reinhart, T. (1984). A surface-structure analysis of "donkey"-anaphora. Ms., Tel Aviv University.

Riemsdijk, H. van, and E. Williams (1981). NP-structure. *The Linguistic Review* 1, 171–217.

Rizzi, L. (1982). Negation, *wh*-movement and the null subject parameter. In *Issues in Italian Syntax*. Foris Publications, Dordrecht.

Ross, J. R. (1967). *Constraints on Variables in Syntax*. Doctoral dissertation, MIT, Cambridge, Mass.

Rouveret, A., and J.-R. Vergnaud (1980). Specifying reference to the subject: French causatives and conditions on representations. *Linguistic Inquiry* 11, 97–202.

Safir, K. (1982). *Syntactic Chains and the Definiteness Effect*. Doctoral dissertation, MIT, Cambridge, Mass.

Safir, K. (1983). On small clauses as constituents. *Linguistic Inquiry* 14, 730–735.

Safir, K. (1984). Multiple variable binding. *Linguistic Inquiry* 15, 603–638.

Sag, I. (1976). *Deletion and Logical Form*. Doctoral dissertation, MIT, Cambridge, Mass.

Schein, B. (1984). Reference to events and quantification. Ms., MIT, Cambridge, Mass.

Stowell, T. (1978). What was there before there was there. In D. Farkas et al., eds., *Proceedings of the Fourteenth Regional Meeting of the Chicago Linguistic Society*. Chicago Linguistic Society, The University of Chicago, Chicago, Ill.

Stowell, T. (1981). *Origins of Phrase Structure*. Doctoral dissertation, MIT, Cambridge, Mass.

Stowell, T. (1983). Subjects across categories. *The Linguistic Review* 2, 285–312.

Thomason, R. (1976). Montague Grammar and some transformations. Ms., University of Pittsburgh, Pittsburgh, Pa.

Toman, J. (1981). Aspects of multiple *wh*-movement in Polish and Czech. In R. May and J. Koster, eds., *Levels of Syntactic Representation*. Foris Publications, Dordrecht.

Williams, E. (1974). *Rule Ordering in Syntax*. Doctoral dissertation, MIT, Cambridge, Mass.

Williams, E. (1977). Discourse and logical form. *Linguistic Inquiry* 8, 101–139.

Williams, E. (1983). Against small clauses. *Linguistic Inquiry* 14, 287–308.

Index